4

ANGEL CLASSICS

# Deutschland

HEINRICH HEINE was born in 1797, into a Jewish family in the Catholic Rhineland. After an unsuccessful attempt to set up in business, he studied law in Bonn, attending A. W. Schlegel's lectures there; Berlin, frequenting Rahel Varnhagen von Ense's celebrated salon where he met leading intellectual figures of the day; and Göttingen, where he took his doctorate in 1825. He was unable to settle to a professional career and uneasy under the repressive German political order of the Metternich era; to these years belong four volumes of travel-writing, *Travel Sketches* (*Reisebilder*, 1826–31). In 1831, attracted by the new dawn of the July Revolution, he moved to Paris, which remained his home for the rest of his life.

Heine began to publish poems while still a student. His first major collection of verse, *Book of Songs* (*Buch der Lieder*, 1827), established his reputation as a lyric poet and was to provide a number of composers, notably Schumann, with song-texts. In Paris Heine lived by his pen, interpreting German life and letters to the French and French politics to the Germans; in Germany his works were officially branded as subversive.

After two last visits to Germany in 1843 and 1844, he published *Germany: A Winter's Tale* (*Deutschland: Ein Wintermärchen*). For the last eight years of his life Heine was confined to what he called a 'mattress grave' by a painful paralytic illness; his last volumes of verse, *Romanzero* (1851) and *Poems 1853 and 1854* (*Gedichte 1853 und 1854*, 1854), contain some of his finest poetry. He died in 1856.

T. J. REED is Taylor Professor of the German Language and Literature at the University of Oxford and Fellow of the Queen's College, and a Fellow of the British Academy. His publications include *Thomas Mann, The Uses of Tradition*, expanded edition Oxford 1996; *The Classical Centre: Goethe and Weimar 1775–1832*, London 1981 and Oxford 1986; volumes on Goethe, 1984 and Schiller, 1991 in the Oxford Past Masters series; and *Making and Unmaking a Master*, a study of Thomas Mann's *Death in Venice*, New York 1994.

HEINRICH HEINE

# Deutschland

*A Winter's Tale*

Bilingual edition

Translation, introduction and notes by
T. J. REED

ANGEL BOOKS
LONDON

First published (without German text) 1986
by Angel Books, 3 Kelross Road, London N5 2QS
Second edition (with German text) published 1997

1 3 5 7 9 10 8 6 4 2

British Library Cataloguing in Publication Data:
A catalogue record for this book is available from the British Library

ISBN 0 946162 58 1

This book is printed on Longlife (acid free) paper conforming to the
British Library recommendations and to the full American standard

Typeset in Great Britain by Trintype (first edition) and
Ray Perry (German text and revised editorial material)

Printed and bound by
Woolnough Bookbinding Ltd, Irthlingborough, Northamptonshire

For Siegbert Prawer

# Contents

# Introduction

Exile is a bitter condition, even for the writer who has been welcomed with open arms by the most stimulating city in Europe. Paris offered Heine a great deal: a social circle of leading writers, artists, politicians, financiers; an audience eager to hear about the latest German poetry and thought; new erotic themes for his own poems. But none of it enough to let the head lie easy:

> I think of Germany in the night,
> and all my sleep is put to flight.
> I cannot get my eyes to close,
> the stream of burning teardrops flows.

He thinks of places he loved, of the culture in which he has his roots, and above all of how his country lies inert in the uneasy calm imposed on Europe after Napoleon's final defeat in 1815. Whatever Napoleon had become – emperor, tyrant, betrayer of the principles of the French Revolution – his fall closed a chapter of European history that had begun in 1789 with high hopes. 'Bliss was it in that dawn to be alive . . . '

Heinrich Heine, born in the Rhineland in 1797, had enjoyed the new freedoms that the Napoleonic occupation paradoxically brought, including, for Jews, exit from the ghetto and the granting of equal rights. But after 1815, the restorers of the old European order led by the Austrian Chancellor Prince Metternich put back the clock, put back thirty-six German princes on their thrones, put back the revolutionary jack-in-the-box and sat on the lid. Heine lived his early manhood under this Restoration, frustrated but intellectually irrepressible, until another seeming new dawn, the July Revolution of 1830, gave him one reason for going to Paris. Not until 1843, after thirteen years of exile, did he go home for a brief visit – in wintry weather, to a country held in Metternich's wintry grip. He duly called the poem that resulted *Germany – A Winter's Tale* (*Deutschland – Ein Wintermärchen*). But it was not a work of resignation. It aimed to bring warmth and light by means of a little friction.

Its first aim is satirical. Heine attacks the backward social and political structures of a country that has never emerged from absolutism, or even in some respects from feudalism. He attacks contemporary culture, especially the Romantic obsession with an idealised Middle Ages, which was keeping the national mind closed to modern alternatives. He points a warning finger at the spread of Prussian power and influence – in 1815 Prussia had acquired his beloved Rhineland – and mocks at Germans for passively letting it happen. The poem's second aim is ideological: to declare new principles on which society could and should be ordered so as to undo the ills and injustices of the present. Among the would-be reformers of his day – some pursuing a national unity beyond the sovereign mini-states for the sake of power and prestige, others the formal guarantees of constitutional monarchy, the franchise, a free press – Heine is closest to the realists who see hunger as the urgent problem and radical change as the unavoidable solution. (At least, he is in principle; he wavers all his life between the demand for social justice at any cost and fear of the egalitarian future.)

But the poem's third and equally important aim is not to get bogged down in the earnestness of the other two. Some contemporaries had; their high principles rang hollow, remained abstract where poetry must be concrete. Their satire also fell short, decrying tyranny without saying who was tyrannising whom and where. As there were thirty-six states, such generalised criticism could always mean somewhere else and the pressure was off. Effective satire has to give chapter and verse and offence. It is the militant arm of the Enlightenment's principle of publicity, according to which nothing that is done can remain wholly unaffected once revealed to the world at large. So satire lives by scandal. As with ideology, tame generalisation was the thing to avoid at all costs.

Heine was well aware of these imperatives. He came to his grand satire on Germany via an earlier satire aimed not at the political evils of the day but at its political poets; and not the poets of any opposed ideology, but those on his own side. They had been pompous, vague and clumsy in handling verse – they had desecrated the poetic art. Heine's mock-epic *Atta Troll* (written 1841–42) pillories them as the dancing bear who escapes from his keeper and returns to his lair in the Pyrenees to preach revolution to the baby bears (animals are the oppressed class, Man the tyrant). Eventually Atta is hunted down, and his pelt ends up beside a Parisian lady's bed, where the poet's bare feet make its acquaintance.

To Heine's wounded colleagues, this seemed perverse and worse. How could any flaws in their poetic performance be more important than the task they were trying to perform? If image and cadence meant more to Heine than principle and purpose, surely he was an unreliable aesthete, a 'talent' without 'character'? But it was not that simple: Heine was living through an inner contradiction. Since early in his career he had written prose works – travel-sketches, journalism, essays in popular cultural and intellectual history – in which political comment and satire were rarely far beneath the dazzlingly varied surface. This had made him a marked man, which was another reason for taking refuge in Paris in 1831. Yet meanwhile his poetry was like the work of another man altogether, a rich reworking of Romantic themes and motifs, touched with irony and disillusion, yet still carrying a torch for poetry as a self-sufficient higher realm. That division and sense of priorities underlay the mockeries of *Atta Troll*.

But irony and disillusion gradually broke down the division between prose and poetry, reality and imagination. Even the earliest and most 'Romantic' of Heine's works, the famous *Book of Songs (Buch der Lieder)* of 1827, is uneasy with its inherited conventions. It has a constant backdrop of woods and hills and meadows, flowers and nightingales, and centre-stage there are Fair Maidens and an Unhappy Lover. (Schumann later reflected all this in the song-settings of *Dichterliebe*.) But a different and harder world waits in the wings, a world of class, money, commerce, and city-dwellers remote from the idyllic countryside, and this other world already affects the language the Lover speaks, which can suddenly ring blasé and colloquial among the conventional prettiness. There are jarring motifs too, mixed in among perfect realisations of Romantic sentiment: vignettes of polite society and its repressed emotions, reminders of how hard up the poet is, bitter hints that his lost love has driven a hard bargain and got herself a better match than this poetic poor relation with whom she apparently once shared some hot feelings.

For a while, in and beyond *Book of Songs*, Heine made emotionally complex poems not from either of these two worlds singly, but from the discomfort of living irresolute between them. This was already a new strand of poetry for modern times, as Baudelaire (who was to continue it) recognised. But even the most resilient poetic imagination cannot easily stay stretched between two worlds. Reality increasingly infiltrates Heine's verse, and that includes political reality. The balladesque lyric 'Tannhäuser' of 1836 (from which Richard Wagner was to derive his operatic subject) begins as a veiled account of Heine's easy life and uneasy conscience in Venusberg-Paris, far from German problems, but ends with a sequence of side-swipes at figures and phenomena on the German scene, linked together only by Tannhäuser's route back from Rome, where the Pope has refused him absolution for living in sin with Venus. It is a small prelude to the full satirical treatment that was to grow out of Heine's own German journey. *Atta Troll* too was, paradoxically, a step in the same direction. Heine might claim that it was art-for-art's-sake as a protest against politicisers, 'perhaps the last free woodland song of Romanticism'. But it was already satire, and thus purposeful; and in the act of mocking other poets' political involvement, it slips into political asides of its

12

own. (Caught in a Pyrenean downpour, the poet outbids Richard III: 'An umbrella! Six-and-thirty kings for an umbrella!') Heine's overt reason for mocking the politicisers might still be that they transgressed his law of poetic purity. But he must also have realised by now that they were damaging the cause he too was committed to. If great social ideas were being made to ring false in public, that was as much a political as a poetic disaster.

Whatever the mixture of motives in Heine (a cynic might add one more: the much-derided political poetry was selling well) by the time he made his journey home in 1843, his poetic talent and his social commitment at last agreed with each other. That does not mean he gave up his allegiance to poetry as a special realm that made special demands. He simply set out to fulfil them in the realm of politics. 'Poetry' was not in the end to be defined by its subject-matter but by its quality: *good* political poetry would be good *poetry*. This was the only logical resolution of his long-lasting inner conflict; and it was equally logical (and a lot more convincing) to answer feeble political poetry with an object-lesson in how to write it, rather than a protest, however witty, against writing it at all. Heine duly announced the new work to his publisher Julius Campe in a letter of April 1844:

> It captures the whole of the present German ferment in the boldest, most personal way. It is politics in the Romantic manner, and I hope it will see off once and for all the leaden bombast of today's would-be political poets. You know I'm not one to boast, but this time I'm sure I've produced a little work that will cause more furore than any popular pamphlet, and yet have the lasting value of a classic poem.

Instant history, critical demolition and literary achievement rolled into one: it was a large claim.

What did Heine's 'little work' capture of pre-1848 Germany, its inertia or 'ferment' (the ferment surely comes from his own intelligence and wit)? At first sight there is more picaresque digression than deep perception, more chance episodes and encounters than coherent design. But

13

where his criticism gets a purchase, an underlying structure shows up: the values Germans accepted or aspired to are a veil (or as Marx would have said, a 'superstructure') for an unpleasant, unavowed reality. Religion and its consolations help to maintain social injustice and make exploitation possible; national unity is pursued at the price of conformity, it has a higher priority than political freedom; patriotism is at root xenophobia, a hatred of the French for past humiliations; the complacent eye that sees the German present as an idyll is ignoring repression and stagnation; sentimental devotion to Germany's cultural past subtly creates resistance to necessary political change in the present, may even hide political purposes which are modern and wholly ruthless. All this is strikingly close to the analysis Marx put forward in the introduction to his *Critique of Hegel's Philosophy of Right*, also dated Paris 1844. That too begins with a (celebrated) attack on religion as the 'opium of the people', an 'upside-down view of the world' that arises because state and society in Germany constitute an 'upside-down world'. Like Heine in Caput I of *Deutschland*, Marx develops his critique of politics and society out of his critique of religion. He also, like Heine, harps on Germany's backwardness. It is an 'anachronism' among the nations of Europe; they have virtually forgotten that such conditions as obtain in Germany can exist, and even the most necessary reforms would barely bring Germany up to the level of 1789. It hardly matters, for our purposes, whether Marx influenced Heine (they had recently met in Paris) or Heine Marx. What the parallels suggest is that Heine was no mere superficial observer or satirical sniper. He has an eye for significant detail, he knows the disease beneath the symptoms. *Deutschland* is a light, but not a lightweight work.

Is it also the classic poem Heine said it would become, disposing of all rivals in the field? Other poets, despite his mockery, had written political poems that were not contemptible, had said things that needed saying and struck stirring notes. But they were the stirring notes of the set-piece political speech, the grand public occasion, with

14

the limited realism that implies. Private man, exhorted to rise to such occasions and be grandly stirred, risks being oversimplified, dwarfed, sometimes even carried away in directions he would rather not go in – it is hardly coincidence that Hoffmann von Fallersleben (see Caput II) wrote Germany's national anthem, a genre not noted for broadening human sympathies. With Heine political poetry takes on a new feel. In place of a rhetorical voice appealing to heightened, slightly unreal listeners, he gives us a personal presence rich in recognisable humanity, keeps it unobtrusively in view as he responds to the changing scenes, weathers and other vicissitudes of travel, and invites us equally to remain our full selves. He treats us to companionable talk, persuasively colloquial rhythms, refreshing wit, irony and self-irony. He draws us into his point of view by the easy tone of a man of the world, first cousin to the Byron of *Don Juan* or the Pushkin of *Eugene Onegin*. So when it comes to satirical skirmishes, we are intuitively on his side, we are at home with this shrewd sardonic mind, the quizzical eye, we sense that his feet are firmly on the ground of experience. We enjoy the marksmanship, identify with the aggression, almost regardless of who or what is being hit. When we look up the historical facts and find that the attack – on censorship, militarism, anti-semitism – was justified, that only confirms what the poetry has already accomplished. Such is the seduction of the first-person narrative – of this particular first person.

If tone and technique do most of this, the plot also helps with its classical, even archetypal simplicity: the exile's return (shades of Ulysses) to an occupied and misruled land; the sense of a mission as he carries his contraband thoughts through customs; the happy arrival home; the epic topos of a final prophetic vision. Legends and symbols fall into place as secret allies: the axeman-double in Cologne; the ominous folktales remembered from the poet's childhood; the dream-meeting with the Emperor Barbarossa, waiting deep in his cave to rise and rescue an abused land. This world of Romantic imagination and allusion is a major source of strength to the poet-traveller. Insofar as Romantic attitudes (false medievalism, excessive attachment to the past) were part of his target, he is turning the enemy's guns round on him. Insofar as he was half a Romantic himself, they were always his guns too. What he was escaping from was the unreality of Romanticism. Here he has adapted Romantic motifs – the *Doppelgänger*, the dream-meeting, a medieval emperor – to real political purposes. That is what is meant by 'politics in the Romantic manner' in the letter to his publisher.

Strength also comes from things of common experience, observed, enjoyed and obscurely felt to be allies too in the political task: German soil underfoot again at last, flooding him with creative power; his mother's love, picking up where it left off years before in immediate concern for his creature comfort; good food and drink; and later on more good food and drink. There are threats too – the Customs, the forest wolves (his suspicious allies), a still painfully active censor, a Prussian fortress-town where dreams of mythical torture ruin his night's sleep. But the balance, as in any comic work – even one with a serious purpose – remains positive, morale rises triumphantly; and as the poem ends with a prophecy of change and a warning to the Prussian King, the movement of Heine's journey has become part of the purposeful movement of history.

Thus the poetic personality and its adventures absorb politics, put it in a human context and an imaginative structure. Even the poet's troubles and uncertainties only enhance his humanity – the dithering over Barbarossa's suitability as an ally, the struggle it costs him to overcome homesickness. None of Heine's contemporaries could match this performance and import individuality into their politics in this 'boldest, most personal way' – none of them *had* this much literary individuality to import, or the nonchalantly brilliant skills to display it at every twist of thought and turn of phrase as Heine does. The sheer humorous accessibility and exuberant play of the poem make it irresistible.

16

Even the ideological opening fanfare of Caput I turns serious doctrine into highly characteristic entertainment. Marx's phrase 'the opium of the people' is telling enough, especially taken out of its context, which is a cluster (not to say clutter) of images. But Heine mounts a coherent unfolding scenario from the moment he hears the emblematic 'musical maiden' at the German frontier, preaching Romantic religiosity. That deceitful lullaby leads on to the hypocrites who exploit the gullibility of the people, then to a programme for feeding all mankind from the generous earth, and a farewell to centuries of asceticism and misery; and finally we witness the wedding celebrated between an allegorical maiden Europe and her suitor Freedom. It is all done with a light touch that steers deftly away from grandiloquence. For example, the problem of hunger means that the grand symbol of 'bread' to feed the masses must be ritually invoked. But is (literal) bread quite enough? Heine had long since decided that men and women needed something beyond basic subsistence, a culture of pleasure and fulfilment, of (as he now puts it) 'roses and myrtles, beauty and joy'. But this is itself starting to sound high-flown, a bit too 'poetic', recalling the shop-steward's vision of idyllic Soviet life in an early Peter Sellers film: 'Fields of waving corn and ballet in the evening'. So Heine brings us back to earth with a quite unsymbolic comestible, specific and succulent: 'and (in the season) peas'. If food is part of the grand doctrine, it can also be a means to keep it real, credible. It does something similar when Heine is eating oranges at his mother's table and answers her inquisitiveness about what party he supports by praising the tasty juice and rejecting the useless peel – the ironist, for better or worse, does not make a party member and sees the organisational means as a distraction from the essential end.

The same flair for keeping a light touch is at work again when Heine abandons a sequence of fierce stanzas that attack some of the villains of his time in what is virtually straight vituperation (see the first Paralipomenon to

Caput XXVI, page 169). However strong his feelings, this was too radical a change from the poem's dominant tone of urbanity. True, the satirist sometimes needs to use 'savage indignation' for his purposes – atrocities, for example, cannot be written about in an urbane, controlled way. But in less extreme cases, it is one of the strengths of satire to stay unruffled, to canalise scorn and hatred and keep to the commanding heights of wit and irony. That is an essential part of the superiority the satirist implicitly claims for himself and his values over the people and systems he attacks. Whatever their power in the real world, within the bounds of his work they are his playthings.

Does all this make *Deutschland* the 'classic poem' Heine intended? In German eyes, it failed to achieve that status for generations. The authorities of course banned it – they would, being its main targets. In fact the Confederation of German States had already banned everything that Heine had written and might write in a decree of 1835; it was only by having a publisher in the Free City of Hamburg that he was able to publish in Germany at all. True, publishers and booksellers had ways of getting things through, and bans even stimulated sales until stocks were actually confiscated as *Deutschland* promptly was, in many places, on grounds of 'blasphemy', 'insubordination' and 'insult to rulers and governments'. There were plenty of Germans who did not take their opinions from the authorities, including socialists whose rising movement needed an alternative literary canon. But the more dutiful burghers were shocked by Heine's irreverence and scurrility – some still are. Their feelings were reflected and confirmed by a peculiar German orthodoxy among critics and academics which has several strands. One is the expectation that great poetry must be simple and inspired, not ironic and reflective. German writers who were noticeably intelligent or (worse) avowedly intellectual, like Lessing or Thomas Mann, have always been made to suffer for it. The poet must also be affirmative rather than questioning and critical; and disfavour grows in proportion as questioning becomes political. 'A nasty song! Ugh! A political song!'

18

bawls one of the drunken students in the tavern scene in Goethe's *Faust*, epitomising Germany's traditionally non-political (that is, in practice politically conservative) culture.

Even where these prejudices were not at work, there was mistrust of anything informal, unsolemn, down-to-earth and (dare one say it?) entertaining. The high classicism of Goethe and Schiller at the historical and psychological centre of German literature, with its commitment to polished form; the deliberate delicate simplicity of the Romantics; the extreme form-consciousness of German aesthetic theory (German eighteenth- and nineteenth-century thinkers virtually invented modern aesthetics): all these built up presumptions about the, in every sense, serious criteria that a would-be classic must fulfil. Satire as such was a dubious candidate, and it would have been positively incongruous to claim classic status for such a seemingly casual, chatty, disrespectful and in places indecent work as Heine's *Deutschland*.

Things have slowly changed. The ideology of the German Democratic Republic and the growth of critical awareness in social matters in the German Federal Republic have undone old taboos (though Heine would not be a comfortable contemporary for his professed admirers on either side of the present German divide). The disasters of modern German history have made satire respectable in hindsight. Aesthetic criteria too have slowly become more flexible. The idea has dawned that to be a classic need not mean formal polish, symmetry and unwavering elevation, but may just as well be a matter of light-footed mobility, mercurial variety, everyday diction, easy-to-read stanzas, the tactics of wit and the strategy of criticism. Heine's work in general and *Deutschland* in particular are now established classics in both Germanies.

But this new recognition, like the old rejection, is only a fact of history. There are also essential reasons, above the ebb and flow of societies, for calling *Deutschland* a classic. Its 'lasting value' (in Heine's words) lies in the exemplary form it gives to a basic human impulse. If the literary canon

19

exists to embrace as full a range of experience as possible, and to enact the appropriate human responses to it so that they are kept in working order, then satire must be there too if we are not to lapse into cultivated passivity. It is there to keep our eyes and our questions sharp and to exercise us in intelligent disrespect. There will always be folly, malice and outrage to require alertness. And the great thing about Heine's poem is the way it links those responses with everyday realities, staying close to the Common Reader and *l'homme moyen sensuel.* Where satire in the grand manner like Alexander Pope's leaves us admiring the elegant syntax and the majestic paired pentameters from afar, Heine draws us into the critical activity.

Is that so very useful though? Criticism can rarely achieve much directly against an authority that can ignore it, censor it or ban it. Certainly satire must not be cast in too heroic, let alone triumphant a role. It cannot bring down the walls of Jericho at a blast of its trumpet; at most it can slowly sap the foundations of blind acceptance and inertia on which the city rests. It can only ever be a prelude to political action, with no guarantee of success – the year of European uprisings in 1848 was a tragic failure (not only were German liberals outmanoeuvred by rulers and their armies, they also showed their own incipient taste for national power rather than civil liberties).

Even in that limited preparatory role, Heine's satire is sometimes condemned for being negative, and having nothing politically constructive to offer us. It is true he gives us no instructions on how to get from principles to realisation – something for which we may need the organisation that his ironic individualism shrank from. Yet his literary and intellectual qualities are themselves valuable politically. His humour alone is a marvellous tonic for morale: it is heartening to hear the voice of sane observation and independence, and to watch the play of superior wit on those grim but never wholly serious things, the powers that be and ought not to be. Heine's very scepticism, too, about some features of politics – the rigidity of party, the woolly talk that reveals woolly thought, the grand gestures that take the place of action – is a useful contribution to sensible politics. As befits a poet, he is concerned with the forms of things, which often turn out to be the key to their substance. Beyond that, what Heine says and the way he says it imply clearly what the Good Society would feel like to live in. Finally, even criticism itself may be more constructive than it seems at first sight. For if society is to be changed, its present shape rather. than some totally new blueprint must be the starting-point; and it takes a sharp eye to see what, beneath superficial appearances, that shape is. As a still young and flexible Karl Marx wrote to Arnold Ruge in 1843, it was 'the advantage of the new direction in politics that we do not dogmatically anticipate the world, but try to find a new world out of the criticism of the old'.

In any case, there is a limit to what one man or type of mind can do. Heine was a poet and satirist, not a political theorist or visionary, and it would be unfair to demand everything of him. The real work is never the satirist's job, but ours.


## Metre, rhythm, rhyme

The stanza Heine uses in *Deutschland* is one of the staple forms found in old German folk ballads and lyrics, such as enthusiasts from the late eighteenth century on had collected. The most famous anthology was Ludwig Achim von Arnim and Clemens Brentano's *Des Knaben Wunderhorn* (*The Boy's Magic Horn*) of 1806–08, which smoothed, roughened, or even pastiched altogether, yet still preserved a great deal that was authentic in form and spirit. Contemporary poets – Brentano, Joseph von Eichendorff, Wilhelm Müller and many others – emulated the old forms in an attempt to achieve the simple poetic speech of folk poetry. Heine in turn, though anything but a simple folk poet, took over these forms along with the rest of the Romantic heritage, and rarely used any others from *Book of Songs* to his death.

21

The *Deutschland* stanza is based on iambic stresses, four each in lines one and three, and three in lines two and four. But the metrical foot is only spasmodically a simple iamb (an unstressed followed by a stressed syllable) because the intervals between stresses can be filled freely with as many light syllables as the reader can be expected to take in his stride, once he is alerted to the colloquial 'naturalness' of the verse. This is the strength of Heine's form, that it can accommodate the stress-sequences actually found in spoken German, in a way the fixed alternation of stressed and unstressed syllables cannot do. The extra syllables, irregularly scattered within the basic beat, infuse life and movement. It is a wonderfully spring-heeled rhythm, ideally suited to a journey and open to virtually any pattern found in speech, yet still held together by the underlying shadow-metre.

That loping movement becomes the hallmark of *Deutschland*, almost a physical gesture (in the sense in which Brecht spoke of gestural language) and part of the poem's meaning: an embodiment of irrepressible humour, ironic query, sardonic defiance or ominous threat. It is not Heine's invention, but he brilliantly exploits for his purpose what was latent in the old folk form: aptly, since he is writing as a tribune of the people in an age when the people are beginning to claim for themselves something more substantial than the curiosity of folklore collectors.

Rhyme also serves Heine's purpose. His more playful and far-fetched rhymes are famous, like Byron's in *Don Juan* ('intellectual/henpeck'd you all'). But even simple rhyme is a powerful ally. Syntax, sense and metre all point to a rendez-vous at the stanza's end; they build up – metre especially, and the more so the more marked its shape and stress patterns – to an expectation of devastation in the last word. To this the sound-echo adds the final touch: when the word lingering in our mind's ear from line two is joined by its partner-in-rhyme at the end of the stanza, three kinds of conclusiveness – syntactical, discursive and aural – coincide, and the poet's statement gains a more than rational authority. How much is lost by not using rhyme (though there are delicate effects of other kinds) is illustrated by Heine's *Atta Troll* stanza. A poem hovering on the brink of politics hovers too in its *Hiawatha*-like metre, never coming down at stanza-endings on a note of decision. Even Atta's onslaughts on the oppressor are left floating in metrical mid-air:

> Humans, are you any better
> than us others, just because your
> skin is smooth and shining? That's a
> feature that you share with serpents.
>
> O Mankind, two-legged serpents,
> I can well perceive the reason
> for your trousers! Wool of others
> covers up your serpent-bareness.

## The text

The first edition of *Deutschland* was published by Hoffmann & Campe in Hamburg in 1844 as a supplement to the volume *New Poems* (*Neue Gedichte*), which brought together all Heine's shorter poems written since *Book of Songs*. This volume, making more than twenty printer's sheets, did not have to undergo censorship (the censorship laws assumed that Short was more likely to be Dangerous). Nevertheless Heine wrote with the authorities in mind, since they could always ban what they had not had a chance to preview. His publisher and other acquaintances then proposed further tonings-down; and Heine made yet further changes off his own bat. Some of the earlier drafts have survived.

Later in the year *Deutschland* was reissued by itself. Being so slight, it had to undergo censorship, even though not a new work, and a number of cuts and changes were required – though not enough to satisfy Prussia, which kept up a campaign of protest until Heine's poor old censor, Hoffmann, was officially reprimanded. (Hammonia is right to say in Caput XXV that he now in his old age 'stretches a point'.)

23

Modern texts of *Deutschland* vary according to whether they follow the first or second edition and whether they use any of the MS drafts. My translation basically follows the first edition, but I have sometimes gone back to a more piquant earlier variant. It would be wrong to try and restore Heine's early text wholesale; not only because the printed text has an obvious authority, but because the revisions forced on him for publication are sometimes more ingenious in their indirectness, or in other ways more effective, than the more explicitly political first drafts. Thus, when prevented in Caput VIII, stanza 7 from saying '*the Prussians*, that scrawny lot', he substituted simply 'the Scrawny Brotherhood'. This subtly builds them (it is plain enough from the context who is meant) into the kind of unpleasant cartoon identity that satire thrives on.

As for stanzas and stanza-sequences that Heine left out altogether, some of these are printed at the end of the present volume as paralipomena. But I have shamelessly conflated the catalogue of the good-time girls of Heine's youth with the usual text of Caput XXIII, for the sheer fun of it. Here, and in one or two other cases of interpolations from Heine's MSS, square brackets will tell the purist when to avert his gaze.

*Postscript, 1997: The German text of the Second Edition*

The German text added in this new edition is based on volume two of Oskar Walzel's edition, *Sämtliche Werke*, Frankfurt am Main 1911ff. Walzel was sensitive to the rhythmic movement that is one of the poem's distinctive features, and restored what he called Heine's own 'declamatory punctuation' (vol. 2, p. 431) and 'intentional peculiarities of orthography' (vol. 2, p. 433, instancing hyphenation and varying elision and non-elision of the letter *e*), as the most accurate guides to Heine's rhythms.

## The translation

The present translation arose by accident, through trying out a few stanzas of a favourite poem when left holding the baby, and getting drawn on. The point of no return was the realisation that rhymes would go on mysteriously turning up. This faith in a divinity that shapes our ends of line entailed not being too demanding, so I have settled for masculine as well as feminine rhymes (Heine's are all feminine) and even on occasion for half-rhyme and assonance. Anything rather than torture the syntax into improbable shapes for the sake of a rhyme, or overwork that sure sign of a verse translation into English, the present participle.

One cannot hope to match Heine's virtuosity, only to catch something of his flavour – tone, manner, gesture. This meant not writing anything that a person of his temperament and convictions could not be imagined saying in English. There are worse ways of coming closer to a writer you enjoy.

Since the baby in question is nearly grown up, the translation has been in the drawer for nearly twice as long as Horace said a work should be left to mature. In the meantime, the American Hal Draper has published his version of Heine's entire poetic works, a heroic undertaking by any standard. But it still seemed worth letting Heine speak with an alternative voice, and offering one of his most appealing works on its own. My original draft has been revised and polished for (and in one or two places by) its present publisher.

The dedication marks the retirement of a distinguished Heine scholar, colleague and friend.

*T. J. Reed*
*St John's College, Oxford*
*July 1986*

25

# Preface to the Second Edition

Since this translation first appeared, Germany has been re-united. Now for the first time Heine has the chance to become a classic in an undivided culture. Under Bismarck and for the rest of the Wilhelmine period, he was rejected as a subversive outsider. That line continued strong in the Weimar Republic. In the Third Reich his Jewishness was enough to put him beyond the pale. In the former German Democratic Republic his place in the literary canon was a niche in a shaky political façade, while in the Federal Republic he was often pressed into a role just as simplistically partisan, with little room left for the full play of his irony. What place the new Germany will give to this passionate defender and outrageous taker of liberties remains to be seen.

The collapse of Germany's second tyranny in this century also brings with it a subtle shift in the way we see a work that took on the repressive regimes of its own day and managed, even as it described the Germany of its title, to imply values that would make a very different country. If the chain reaction of modern German history is now, as it seems, finally burned out, Heine's poem no longer speaks with the voice of one of history's losers, first side'ined by seemingly triumphal events and then overshadowed by their tragic consequences. His principles and energy, his sharp eye and his still sharper pen, become an example and a resource for an open society. The bicentenary of Heine's birth, about to be celebrated as this new edition goes to press, could not have fallen at a better time.

*T. J. Reed*
*The Queen's College, Oxford*
*April 1997*

# Deutschland

*A Winter's Tale*

# I

Im traurigen Monat November wars,
Die Tage wurden trüber,
Der Wind riß von den Bäumen das Laub,
Da reist ich nach Deutschland hinüber.

Und als ich an die Grenze kam,
Da fühlt ich ein stärkeres Klopfen
In meiner Brust, ich glaube sogar
Die Augen begunnen zu tropfen.

Und als ich die deutsche Sprache vernahm,
Da ward mir seltsam zu Mute;
Ich meinte nicht anders, als ob das Herz
Recht angenehm verblute.

Ein kleines Harfenmädchen sang.
Sie sang mit wahrem Gefühle
Und falscher Stimme, doch ward ich sehr
Gerühret von ihrem Spiele.

Sie sang von Liebe und Liebesgram,
Aufopfrung und Wiederfinden
Dort oben, in jener besseren Welt,
Wo alle Leiden schwinden.

Sie sang vom irdischen Jammertal,
Von Freuden, die bald zerronnen,
Vom Jenseits, wo die Seele schwelgt
Verklärt in ewgen Wonnen.

Sie sang das alte Entsagungslied,
Das Eiapopeia vom Himmel,
Womit man einlullt, wenn es greint,
Das Volk, den großen Lümmel.

# I

In the dismal month of November it was,
the gloomy days grew shorter,
the wind was tugging the last leaves down
as I left for the German border.

And as I came nearer German soil,
I felt my heart beat quicker
within my breast, and I even think
a tear began to trickle.

It did strange things to me when I heard
the German language spoken –
like nothing so much as if my heart
was pleasantly being broken.

A little girl was playing the harp
and singing with genuine feeling
and out of tune, but still the song
she sang was most appealing.

She sang of love and sacrifice,
of pain and a tomorrow
when all shall meet in a better world
beyond this vale of sorrow;

of how all sufferings will be past,
each soul will bask transfigured
in joys eternal, not like here
where pleasures are brief and niggard.

She sang the ancient lullaby
of doing without, of pie-in-
the-sky, that they soothe the people with,
great oaf, when they hear it crying.

29

Ich kenne die Weise, ich kenne den Text,
Ich kenn auch die Herren Verfasser;
Ich weiß, sie tranken heimlich Wein
Und predigten öffentlich Wasser.

Ein neues Lied, ein besseres Lied,
O Freunde, will ich Euch dichten!
Wir wollen hier auf Erden schon
Das Himmelreich errichten.

Wir wollen auf Erden glücklich sein,
Und wollen nicht mehr darben;
Verschlemmen soll nicht der faule Bauch
Was fleißige Hände erwarben.

Es wächst hienieden Brot genug
Für alle Menschenkinder,
Auch Rosen und Myrten, Schönheit und Lust,
Und Zuckererbsen nicht minder.

Ja, Zuckererbsen für jedermann,
Sobald die Schoten platzen!
Den Himmel überlassen wir
Den Engeln und den Spatzen.

Und wachsen uns Flügel nach dem Tod,
So wollen wir Euch besuchen
Dort oben, und wir, wir essen mit Euch
Die seligsten Torten und Kuchen.

Ein neues Lied, ein besseres Lied,
Es klingt wie Flöten und Geigen!
Das Miserere ist vorbei,
Die Sterbeglocken schweigen.

Die Jungfer Europa ist verlobt
Mit dem schönen Geniusse
Der Freiheit, sie liegen einander im Arm,
Sie schwelgen im ersten Kusse.

I know the tune, I know the words,
I know every single author;
I know they tippled wine on the quiet
while publicly preaching water.

A different song, a better song,
will get the subject straighter:
let's make a heaven on earth, my friends,
instead of waiting till later.

Why shouldn't we be happy on earth,
why should we still go short?
Why should the idle belly consume
what working hands have wrought?

There's bread enough grows here on earth
to feed mankind with ease,
and roses and myrtles, beauty and joy,
and (in the season) peas.

Yes, fresh green peas for everyone
as soon as the pods have burst.
Heaven we'll leave to the angels, and
the sparrows, who had it first.

And should we find that after death
we've grown some wings, we'll make
a point of calling on you up there
for some blessèd tea-and-cake.

A better song, with fiddles and flutes,
to set the people singing!
The miserere is out of date,
the death-knell's no longer ringing.

The maiden Europa is betrothed
to that handsome Genius, Freedom.
They lie in each other's arms embraced,
it warms my heart to see them.

Und fehlt der Pfaffensegen dabei,
Die Ehe wird gültig nicht minder –
Es lebe Bräutigam und Braut,
Und ihre zukünftigen Kinder!

Ein Hochzeitkarmen ist mein Lied,
Das bessere, das neue!
In meiner Seele gehen auf
Die Sterne der höchsten Weihe –

Begeisterte Sterne, sie lodern wild,
Zerfließen in Flammenbächen –
Ich fühle mich wunderbar erstarkt,
Ich könnte Eichen zerbrechen!

Seit ich auf deutsche Erde trat,
Durchströmen mich Zaubersäfte –
Der Riese hat wieder die Mutter berührt,
Und es wuchsen ihm neu die Kräfte.


II

Während die Kleine von Himmelslust
Getrillert und musizieret,
Ward von den preußischen Douaniers
Mein Koffer visitieret.

Beschnüffelten Alles, kramten herum
In Hemden, Hosen, Schnupftüchern;
Sie suchten nach Spitzen, nach Bijouterien,
Auch nach verbotenen Büchern.

Ihr Toren, die Ihr im Koffer sucht!
Hier werdet Ihr nichts entdecken!
Die Contrebande, die mit mir reist,
Die hab ich im Kopfe stecken.

No priest will bless their vows, but the pair
have taken and will fulfil them.
Here's to the bride and here's to the groom,
and to all their future children.

That's wedding enough, and I'll sing my song
to help the solemnising.
Deep in my heart I feel the stars
of consecration rising.

They are stars inspired, they wildly glow,
Dissolving in streams of fire –
I feel I could break an oak, my strength
miraculously grows higher.

Since I set foot on German soil
the magic juices are flowing –
the giant has touched his mother again,
and he feels his powers growing.


II


While that musical maiden warbled about
her heavenly predilection,
the Prussian Customs gave my trunk
the usual prying inspection.

They sniffed and rummaged in shirts and pants
to see if I'd something hidden –
jewels, or Belgian lace, or books
the censor had forbidden.

It's no good poking about, you fools,
peering and looking worried.
The contraband is not in there,
it's safe behind my forehead.

Hier hab ich Spitzen, die feiner sind
Als die von Brüssel und Mecheln,
Und pack ich einst meine Spitzen aus,
Sie werden euch sticheln und hecheln.

Im Kopfe trage ich Bijouterien,
Der Zukunft Krondiamanten,
Die Tempelkleinodien des neuen Gotts,
Des großen Unbekannten.

Und viele Bücher trag ich im Kopf!
Ich darf es Euch versichern,
Mein Kopf ist ein zwitscherndes Vogelnest
Von konfiszierlichen Büchern.

Glaubt mir, in Satans Bibliothek
Kann es nicht schlimmere geben;
Sie sind gefährlicher noch als die
Von Hoffmann von Fallersleben! –

Ein Passagier, der neben mir stand,
Bemerkte mir, ich hätte
Jetzt vor mir den preußischen Zollverein,
Die große Douanenkette.

»Der Zollverein« – bemerkte er –
»Wird unser Volkstum begründen,
Er wird das zersplitterte Vaterland
Zu einem Ganzen verbinden.

»Er gibt die äußere Einheit uns,
Die sogenannt materielle;
Die geistige Einheit gibt uns die Zensur,
Die wahrhaft ideelle –

»Sie gibt die innere Einheit uns,
Die Einheit im Denken und Sinnen;
Ein einiges Deutschland tut uns not,
Einig nach Außen und Innen.«

I've something that needles of Malines
and Brussels could not work finer.
You'll find when *my* needles get to work
They're sharper and maligner.

And jewels are there, crown jewels, no less,
of ages that will succeed us,
temple jewels for an unknown god
when from the old one he's freed us.

And books! I'm full of them, like a tree
in spring when the songbirds have nested
and fledglings clamour to take the wing –
any one would get me arrested.

You'd not find books on Satan's shelves
of upheaval more precursive.
That Hoffmann von Fallersleben chap
hasn't been more subversive.

Another passenger standing near
remarked that what I was seeing
was the famous Prussian Zollverein,
the Great Chain of Well-being.

'The Customs Union,' he opined,
'will be our people's foundation,
and make the divided fatherland
into a single nation.

'This outward unity is our first
since the empire of you-know-when, sir.
The higher unity of ideas
is the task we leave to the censor.

'Yes, inner unity is his job,
we must all think as he allows us.
Germany one, without and within –
that's the ideal to rouse us.'

# III

Zu Aachen, im alten Dome, liegt
Carolus Magnus begraben.
(Man muß ihn nicht verwechseln mit Karl
Mayer, der lebt in Schwaben.)

Ich möchte nicht tot und begraben sein
Als Kaiser zu Aachen im Dome;
Weit lieber lebt ich als kleinster Poet
Zu Stukkert am Neckarstrome.

Zu Aachen langweilen sich auf der Straß
Die Hunde, sie flehn untertänig:
Gib uns einen Fußtritt, o Fremdling, das wird
Vielleicht uns zerstreuen ein wenig.

Ich bin in diesem langweilgen Nest
Ein Stündchen herumgeschlendert.
Sah wieder preußisches Militär,
Hat sich nicht sehr verändert.

Es sind die grauen Mäntel noch
Mit dem hohen, roten Kragen –
(Das Rot bedeutet Franzosenblut,
Sang Körner in früheren Tagen.)

Noch immer das hölzern pedantische Volk,
Noch immer ein rechter Winkel
In jeder Bewegung, und im Gesicht
Der eingefrorene Dünkel.

Sie stelzen noch immer so steif herum,
So kerzengrade geschniegelt,
Als hätten sie verschluckt den Stock,
Womit man sie einst geprügelt.

# III

The bones of Carolus Magnus lie
in Aachen cathedral (maybe a
bit confusing, I don't mean wee
Karl Mayer, he lives in Swabia.)

I wouldn't much like to be buried, for all
that splendid imperial shrining.
I'd rather be living, even down there
in Stuttgart, mis'rably rhyming.

The Aachen dogs are so bored, their tails
implore you with servile wagging:
'Give us a kick, o stranger, perhaps
it'll stop our interest flagging.'

I walked about in that boring hole
for an hour or more together.
I saw the Prussian soldiers again.
They're still the same as ever.

Still the same grey coats, and still
the high and blood-red collar
('The red is for the Frenchies' blood,'
as Körner used to holler).

They're still a wooden pedantic lot,
their movements still have the graces
of a right-angled triangle.
Arrogance freezes their faces.

And still they strut about as stiff,
as straight and thin as a candle,
as if they'd swallowed the corporal's stick
Old Fritz knew how to handle.

Ja, ganz verschwand die Fuchtel nie,
Sie tragen sie jetzt im Innern;
Das trauliche Du wird immer noch
An das alte Er erinnern.

Der lange Schnurrbart ist eigentlich nur
Des Zopftums neuere Phase:
Der Zopf, der ehmals hinten hing,
Der hängt jetzt unter der Nase.

Nicht übel gefiel mir das neue Kostüm
Der Reuter, das muß ich loben,
Besonders die Pickelhaube, den Helm,
Mit der stählernen Spitze nach oben.

Das ist so rittertümlich und mahnt
An der Vorzeit holde Romantik,
An die Burgfrau Johanna von Montfaucon,
An den Freiherrn Fouqué, Uhland, Tieck.

Das mahnt an das Mittelalter so schön,
An Edelknechte und Knappen,
Die in dem Herzen getragen die Treu
Und auf dem Hintern ein Wappen.

Das mahnt an Kreuzzug und Turnei,
An Minne und frommes Dienen,
An die ungedruckte Glaubenszeit,
Wo noch keine Zeitung erschienen.

Ja, ja, der Helm gefällt mir, er zeugt
Vom allerhöchsten Witze!
Ein königlicher Einfall wars!
Es fehlt nicht die Pointe, die Spitze!

Nur fürcht ich, wenn ein Gewitter entsteht,
Zieht leicht so eine Spitze
Herab auf Euer romantisches Haupt
Des Himmels modernste Blitze! – –

The stick has never quite been lost,
although its use has been banned.
Inside the glove of newer ways
there's still the old iron hand.

The long moustache is the pigtail of old,
transferred to a different place.
The pigtail once hung down behind,
now it droops from the face.

The cavalry's new get-up I quite
approved – one must speak fairly –
especially that spike of steel
which crowns it all so squarely,

so redolent of derring-do,
of knights in times Romantic,
of Lady Jane of Falconmount
and m'lords Fouqué, Uhland, Tieck;

Of the good olde Middle Ages so fine,
of pages and noble peers,
who bore in their hearts a trust right true,
and coats of arms on their rears.

Crusade and tourney it conjures up,
and serving a lady for guerdon,
an age of faith without blessing of print,
when newspapers hadn't been heard on.

Oh yes, I like the helmet, it proves
the wit of the Lord's Anointed!
A royal jest it was indeed,
most delicately pointed.

It's really only the thought of storms
that I find a little fright'ning –
that spike on your Romantic heads
might attract some modern lightning.

[Und wenn es Krieg gibt, müßt Ihr Euch
Viel leichteres Kopfzeug kaufen,
Des Mittelalters schwerer Helm
Könnt Euch genieren im Laufen.]


Zu Aachen, auf dem Posthausschild,
Sah ich den Vogel wieder,
Der mir so tief verhaßt! Voll Gift
Schaute er auf mich nieder.


Du häßlicher Vogel, wirst du einst
Mir in die Hände fallen,
So rupfe ich dir die Federn aus
Und hacke dir ab die Krallen.


Du sollst mir dann, in luftger Höh,
Auf einer Stange sitzen,
Und ich rufe zum lustigen Schießen herbei
Die Rheinischen Vogelschützen.


Wer mir den Vogel herunterschießt,
Mit Zepter und Krone belehn ich
Den wackern Mann! Wir blasen Tusch
Und rufen: es lebe der König!


IV


Zu Cöllen kam ich spät Abends an,
Da hörte ich rauschen den Rheinfluß,
Da fächelte mich schon deutsche Luft,
Da fühlt ich ihren Einfluß –


Auf meinen Appetit. Ich aß
Dort Eierkuchen mit Schinken,
Und da er sehr gesalzen war,
Mußt ich auch Rheinwein trinken.

[And when it comes to war, perhaps
you'll have to get something lighter:
the weight of the Middle Ages might
weigh down a fleeing fighter.]

At Aachen I saw that bird I hate
displayed on the staging sign;
back at me he looked with an eye
most poisonously malign.

You ugly devil, just you wait,
if ever I manage to catch you
I'll pluck out your feathers and hack off your claws
and then as follows despatch you:

I'll set you up on top of a pole
high in the air as a target,
and all the Rhineland marksmen shall come
for a jolly shooting party.

The man who brings you down, I shall
in person sceptre-and-crown him –
the worthy fellow! A fanfare shall blow,
and vivats shall ring all around him.


IV


It was getting late when we reached Cologne;
the Rhine was whispering fondly,
my cheeks were fanned by German air,
I felt its influence on me –

on my appetite, that is. I ate
ham omelette, and as my portion
was rather salty, I had to drink
some hock as a precaution.

41

Der Rheinwein glänzt noch immer wie Gold
Im grünen Römerglase,
Und trinkst du etwelche Schoppen zu viel,
So steigt er dir in die Nase.

In die Nase steigt ein Prickeln so süß,
Man kann sich vor Wonne nicht lassen!
Es trieb mich hinaus in die dämmernde Nacht,
In die widerhallenden Gassen.

Die steinernen Häuser schauten mich an,
Als wollten sie mir berichten
Legenden aus altverschollener Zeit,
Der heilgen Stadt Cöllen Geschichten.

Ja, hier hat einst die Klerisei
Ihr frommes Wesen getrieben,
Hier haben die Dunkelmänner geherrscht,
Die Ulrich von Hutten beschrieben.

Der Cancan des Mittelalters ward hier
Getanzt von Nonnen und Mönchen;
Hier schrieb Hochstraaten, der Menzel von Cöln,
Die giftgen Denunziaziönchen.

Die Flamme des Scheiterhaufens hat hier
Bücher und Menschen verschlungen;
Die Glocken wurden geläutet dabei
Und Kyrie Eleison gesungen.

Dummheit und Bosheit buhlten hier
Gleich Hunden auf freier Gasse;
Die Enkelbrut erkennt man noch heut
An ihrem Glaubenshasse. –

Doch siehe! dort im Mondenschein
Den kolossalen Gesellen!
Er ragt verteufelt schwarz empor,
Das ist der Dom von Cöllen.

42

When you hold it up in its green-stemmed glass
the golden hock still glows,
and if you fill up too many times
it begins to tickle your nose.

A prickling tickling sweet delight,
you can hardly keep your seat.
It drove me out in the dusky night
to pace the echoing street.

As I walked about, I seemed to hear
the ancient houses of stone
recounting tales of bygone days,
the legends of holy Cologne.

It was once a centre of clerisy
and the pious things they engage in.
It was here the Men Obscure held sway
who set Ulrich von Hutten raging.

Here monks and nuns did their cancan, and here
Hochstraaten poured his venom
into denunciatory notes.
(Today we have Menzel to pen 'em.)

It was here the flames of pious fires
burnt books and men to ashes.
They rang the bells meanwhile, and prayed
for the Lord to have compassion.

Here malice and stupidity
like curs in the roadway mated.
You can tell their progeny still today
by their theological hatred.

But look! there in the white of the moon
something colossal towers.
That's the cathedral of Cologne,
black as the devilish powers.

Er sollte des Geistes Bastille sein,
Und die listigen Römlinge dachten:
In diesem Riesenkerker wird
Die deutsche Vernunft verschmachten!

Da kam der Luther, und er hat
Sein großes »Halt!« gesprochen –
Seit jenem Tage blieb der Bau
Des Domes unterbrochen.

Er ward nicht vollendet – und das ist gut.
Denn eben die Nichtvollendung
Macht ihn zum Denkmal von Deutschlands Kraft
Und protestantischer Sendung.

Ihr armen Schelme vom Domverein,
Ihr wollt mit schwachen Händen
Fortsetzen das unterbrochene Werk
Und die alte Zwingburg vollenden!

O törichter Wahn! Vergebens wird
Geschüttelt der Klingelbeutel,
Gebettelt bei Ketzern und Juden sogar;
Ist alles fruchtlos und eitel.

Vergebens wird der große Franz Liszt
Zum Besten des Doms musizieren,
Und ein talentvoller König wird
Vergebens deklamieren!

Er wird nicht vollendet, der Cölner Dom,
Obgleich die Narren in Schwaben
Zu seinem Fortbau ein ganzes Schiff
Voll Steine gesendet haben.

Er wird nicht vollendet, trotz allem Geschrei
Der Raben und der Eulen,
Die, altertümlich gesinnt, so gern
In hohen Kirchtürmen weilen.

It was meant to be the mind's Bastille –
the papists wanted a prison
in whose enormous vaults to lock
forever German reason.

Then Luther came, by whose mighty 'Stay'
the work was interrupted –
since when Cologne cathedral has
remained but half-constructed.

It was never completed – an excellent thing,
for its very non-completion
is a monument to Germany's strength
and Germany's protestant mission.

Poor rascals of the Cathedral Trust,
it's a task beyond your powers
to carry through that dark design
and raise those unfinished towers.

O farcical dream! In vain you shake
the box, in vain you've collected
from Jews, of all people, and heretics:
still nothing will get erected.

The great Franz Liszt himself may play
to boost your building balance,
and on your behalf a certain king
may display his rhetorical talents.

It won't be built, it'll never get done,
though the Swabians were so daft
as to send their gift of a ship packed full
with stone from fore to aft.

It won't get finished, for all the din
from those blinking owls and ravens –
such creatures of out-dated tastes
find church-towers ideal havens.

Ja, kommen wird die Zeit sogar,
Wo man, statt ihn zu vollenden,
Die inneren Räume zu einem Stall
Für Pferde wird verwenden.

»Und wird der Dom ein Pferdestall,
Was sollen wir dann beginnen
Mit den heilgen drei Köngen, die da ruhn
Im Tabernakel da drinnen?«

So höre ich fragen. Doch brauchen wir uns
In unserer Zeit zu genieren?
Die heilgen drei Könge aus Morgenland,
Sie können wo anders logieren.

Folgt meinem Rat und steckt sie hinein
In jene drei Körbe von Eisen,
Die hoch zu Münster hängen am Turm,
Der Sankt Lamberti geheißen.

Der Schneiderkönig saß darin
Mit seinen beiden Räten,
Wir aber benutzen die Körbe jetzt
Für andre Majestäten.

Zur Rechten soll Herr Balthasar,
Zur Linken Herr Melchior schweben,
In der Mitte Herr Gaspar – Gott weiß, wie einst
Die Drei gehaust im Leben!

Die heilge Allianz des Morgenlands,
Die jetzt kanonisieret,
Sie hat vielleicht nicht immer schön
Und fromm sich aufgeführet.

Der Balthasar und der Melchior,
Das waren vielleicht zwei Gäuche,
Die in der Not eine Konstitution
Versprochen ihrem Reiche,

In fact, I even foresee one day
a better proposal than yours is.
The cathedral innards will be cleared
to make a stable for horses.

'A stable? But where shall our relics be put,
from time immemorial dating,
the bones of the Three Wise Men, no less?
They'll need accommodating.'

Such is the question. But nowadays
do we need to be so formal?
Put your three kings up somewhere else,
a change of address is quite normal.

Take my advice, and hang them up
in those three iron cages
that have hung in Münster on the tower
of St Lambert's church for ages.

The Tailor-King and his Councillors
once hung there in wind and weather;
we'll use the baskets now for diff-
erent majesties altogether.

We'll set Lord Balthasar on the right,
on the left Lord Melchior swinging,
Lord Caspar between 'em – God knows what deeds
they perpetrated when living.

The Holy Alliance of the East,
though canonised now, may not 've
been better by much than the modern three,
whose bad side we've seen such a lot of.

Old Balthasar and Melchior
may have been the kind of princes
who promise a constitution, just
as long as emergency pinches,

Und später nicht Wort gehalten – Es hat
Herr Gaspar, der König der Mohren,
Vielleicht mit schwarzem Undank sogar
Belohnt sein Volk, die Toren!

[Fehlt etwa einer vom Triumvirat,
So nehmt einen anderen Menschen,
Ersetzt den König des Morgenlands
Durch einen abendländschen.]


## V


Und als ich an die Rheinbrück kam,
Wohl an die Hafenschanze,
Da sah ich fließen den Vater Rhein
Im stillen Mondenglanze.

Sei mir gegrüßt, mein Vater Rhein,
Wie ist es dir ergangen?
Ich habe oft an dich gedacht
Mit Sehnsucht und Verlangen.

So sprach ich, da hört ich im Wasser tief
Gar seltsam grämliche Töne,
Wie Hüsteln eines alten Manns,
Ein Brümmeln und weiches Gestöhne:

»Willkommen, mein Junge, das ist mir lieb,
Daß du mich nicht vergessen;
Seit dreizehn Jahren sah ich dich nicht,
Mir ging es schlecht unterdessen.

»Zu Biberich hab ich Steine verschluckt,
Wahrhaftig, sie schmeckten nicht lecker!
Doch schwerer liegen im Magen mir
Die Verse von Niklas Becker.

Then break their word. And maybe too
King Caspar, the Moorish lord,
gave only black ingratitude
as his foolish subjects' reward.

[So if you should happen to lose on the way
one of those kings oriental,
why not hang high a specimen
of a modern one, occidental?]


V


On I walked, and came to the bridge
down by the harbour at last;
in the tranquil moonlight Father Rhine
was slowly flowing past.

'Greetings to you, my Father Rhine,
how are things with you and yours?
There have been times when I yearned to be
back here upon your shores.'

Thus I spoke. From the watery depths
came a strange and petulant moaning,
as if an old man was clearing his throat,
rumbling and feebly groaning.

'Welcome, my boy, it's nice to feel
that I haven't been forgotten.
I haven't seen you for thirteen years;
things have been pretty rotten.

'At Bieberich I swallowed some stones,
they made my digestion much worse;
but what I found harder to stomach still
was Niklas Becker's verse.

»Er hat mich besungen, als ob ich noch
Die reinste Jungfer wäre,
Die sich von niemand rauben läßt
Das Kränzlein ihrer Ehre.

»Wenn ich es höre, das dumme Lied,
Dann möcht ich mir zerraufen
Den weißen Bart, ich möchte fürwahr
Mich in mir selbst ersaufen!

Daß ich keine reine Jungfer bin,
Die Franzosen wissen es besser,
Sie haben mit meinem Wasser so oft
Vermischt ihr Siegergewässer.

»Das dumme Lied und der dumme Kerl!
Er hat mich schmählich blamieret,
Gewissermaßen hat er mich auch
Politisch kompromittieret.

»Denn kehren jetzt die Franzosen zurück,
So muß ich vor ihnen erröten,
Ich, der um ihre Rückkehr so oft
Mit Tränen zum Himmel gebeten.

»Ich habe sie immer so lieb gehabt,
Die lieben kleinen Französchen –
Singen und springen sie noch wie sonst?
Tragen noch weiße Höschen?

»Ich möchte sie gerne wiedersehn,
Doch fürcht ich die Persiflage,
Von wegen des verwünschten Lieds,
Von wegen der Blamage.

»Der Alfred de Musset, der Gassenbub,
Der kommt an ihrer Spitze
Vielleicht als Tambour, und trommelt mir vor
All seine schlechten Witze.«

'His poem made me out to be
the purest *virgo intacta*,
defending her honour valiantly
against anyone who attacked her.

'I could tear my beard in fury when
I hear his silly poem.
I wish I could drown myself in myself,
but I have to keep on flowing.

'Me a virgin? The French would laugh!
My water's adulterated
from all the battles they've won on my banks,
then festively urinated.

'What a silly song! What a silly chap!
I find it all most harassing.
He's also made my position here
politically embarrassing.

'Just reflect! If the French came back,
I'd blush for shame before them –
Though I've prayed to God for all these years
that he would kindly restore them.

'I had a soft spot for those little chaps –
you know how their charm bewitches.
Do they still sing and prance about?
Do they still wear the same white breeches?

'I'd really love to see them again,
except I'm afraid of their mockery
because of that Becker's accursed song
that made a laughing-stock o'me.

'That urchin Alfred de Musset, you'll see,
will drum at the head of their column.
He'll pound out all his rotten jokes
(well, jokes the Frenchies call 'em).'

So klagte der arme Vater Rhein,
Konnt sich nicht zufrieden geben.
Ich sprach zu ihm manch tröstendes Wort,
Um ihm das Herz zu heben:

O fürchte nicht, mein Vater Rhein,
Den spöttelnden Scherz der Franzosen;
Sie sind die alten Franzosen nicht mehr,
Auch tragen sie andere Hosen.

Die Hosen sind rot und nicht mehr weiß,
Sie haben auch andere Knöpfe,
Sie singen nicht mehr, sie springen nicht mehr,
Sie senken nachdenklich die Köpfe.

Sie philosophieren und sprechen jetzt
Von Kant, von Fichte und Hegel,
Sie rauchen Tabak, sie trinken Bier,
Und manche schieben auch Kegel.

Sie werden Philister ganz wie wir
Und treiben es endlich noch ärger;
Sie sind keine Voltairianer mehr,
Sie werden Hengstenberger.

Der Alfred de Musset, das ist wahr,
Ist noch ein Gassenjunge;
Doch fürchte nichts, wir fesseln ihm
Die schändliche Spötterzunge.

Und trommelt er dir einen schlechten Witz,
So pfeifen wir ihm einen schlimmern,
Wir pfeifen ihm vor, was ihm passiert
Bei schönen Frauenzimmern.

Gib dich zufrieden, Vater Rhein,
Denk nicht an schlechte Lieder,
Ein besseres Lied vernimmst du bald –
Leb wohl, wir sehen uns wieder.

Thus ran old Father Rhine's lament.
Nothing I said consoled him.
But so as to cheer him up a bit,
this was what I told him:

'Never fear, old Father Rhine,
there have recently been some hitches;
the French are not the wits they were,
they also wear different breeches.

'Their breeches are red and no longer white,
they also have different buttons;
singing and prancing are out – they've returned
to their metaphysical muttons.

'They're philosophers now, their talk is Kant
and Hegel and such-like names;
they smoke tobacco, they all drink beer
and some play our beer-house games.

'They're becoming philistines just like us,
in fact, their behaviour's extremer.
They don't think much of Voltaire any more,
he wasn't a German dreamer.

'That Alfred de Musset, I must admit,
is still a saucy urchin;
but never fear, we'll see his tongue
doesn't do any shameful besmirching.

'If he drums you one of his rotten jokes,
we'll pipe back, to show we can take it,
the tale of all the women he's chased,
without ever seeming to make it.

'Old Father Rhine, don't let the thought
of that stupid poem daunt ye.
Soon I'll sing you a better song.
Farewell now, we'll meet again shortly.'

Den Paganini begleitete stets
Ein Spiritus Familiaris,
Manchmal als Hund, manchmal in Gestalt
Des seligen Georg Harris.

Napoleon sah einen roten Mann
Vor jedem wichtgen Ereignis.
Sokrates hatte seinen Dämon,
Das war kein Hirnerzeugnis.

Ich selbst, wenn ich am Schreibtisch saß
Des Nachts, hab ich gesehen
Zuweilen einen vermummten Gast
Unheimlich hinter mir stehen.

Unter dem Mantel hielt er etwas
Verborgen, das seltsam blinkte,
Wenn es zum Vorschein kam, und ein Beil,
Ein Richtbeil, zu sein mir dünkte.

Er schien von untersetzter Statur,
Die Augen wie zwei Sterne;
Er störte mich im Schreiben nie,
Blieb ruhig stehn in der Ferne.

Seit Jahren hatte ich nicht gesehn
Den sonderbaren Gesellen,
Da fand ich ihn plötzlich wieder hier
In der stillen Mondnacht zu Cöllen.

Ich schlenderte sinnend die Straßen entlang,
Da sah ich ihn hinter mir gehen,
Als ob er mein Schatten wäre, und stand
Ich still, so blieb er stehen.

## VI

They say Paganini was never without
a *spiritus familiaris*,
now in the shape of a dog, and now
in the shape of the late George Harris.

Napoleon saw a crimson man
when events were in the making;
Socrates had his daemon too –
the great man wasn't faking.

I myself, when I've sat down to write,
at night have sometimes noticed
a guest, uncanny, with face obscured,
behind my desk-chair posted.

Underneath his cloak he held
something concealed that glinted,
an axe, an executioner's axe –
or so my glimpse of it hinted.

He seemed to be of stocky build,
his eyes like stars shone brightly.
He never disturbed my writing, though,
he kept his distance politely.

This strange nocturnal visitor
for years had left me alone.
Suddenly there he was again
in the moonlight in quiet Cologne.

I was strolling musing through the streets
when I saw him behind me pacing;
he stopped when I did, shadow-like,
ever my footsteps tracing,

Blieb stehen, als wartete er auf was,
Und förderte ich die Schritte,
Dann folgte er wieder. So kamen wir
Bis auf des Domplatz Mitte.

Es ward mir unleidlich, ich drehte mich um
Und sprach: Jetzt steh mir Rede,
Was folgst du mir auf Weg und Steg,
Hier in der nächtlichen Öde?

Ich treffe dich immer in der Stund,
Wo Weltgefühle sprießen
In meiner Brust und durch das Hirn
Die Geistesblitze schießen.

Du siehst mich an so stier und fest –
Steh Rede: was verhüllst du
Hier unter dem Mantel, das heimlich blinkt?
Wer bist du und was willst du?

Doch jener erwiderte trockenen Tons,
Sogar ein bißchen phlegmatisch:
»Ich bitte dich, exorziere mich nicht,
Und werde nur nicht emphatisch!

»Ich bin kein Gespenst der Vergangenheit,
Kein grabentstiegener Strohwisch,
Und von Rhetorik bin ich kein Freund,
Bin auch nicht sehr philosophisch.

»Ich bin von praktischer Natur,
Und immer schweigsam und ruhig.
Doch wisse: was du ersonnen im Geist,
Das führ ich aus, das tu ich.

»Und gehn auch Jahre drüber hin,
Ich raste nicht, bis ich verwandle
In Wirklichkeit was du gedacht;
Du denkst, und ich, ich handle.

stopped as if waiting for something, then
came on when the pace grew stronger
until we reached the Cathedral Square
and I could stand it no longer.

I turned about and faced him there:
'All right,' I said, 'what *is* this?
Pursuing me through the deserted night
as I go about my business?

'I always meet you in the hour
when mighty emotions are swelling
within my breast, and my mind flashes forth
ideas at their most compelling.

'You stare at me with such piercing gaze –
now stand and tell me truly:
what is it that glints there beneath your cloak,
who are you and why d'you pursue me?'

But he replied in a dryish tone,
you might almost say phlegmatic:
'Now don't go exorcising me,
and pray don't get emphatic.

'I'm not a phantom from the past,
nor a wraith whose tombstone has lifted,
I'm not inclined to rhetoric
nor philosophic'lly gifted.

'My disposition is practical,
silence and calmness suit it.
But know: what you conceive in your mind,
I do it, I execute it.

'Years may go by, but I do not rest
till I've transformed the abstraction
into reality. Your sphere
is thought, and mine is action.

»Du bist der Richter, der Büttel bin ich,
Und mit dem Gehorsam des Knechtes
Vollstreck ich das Urteil, das du gefällt,
Und sei es ein ungerechtes.

»Dem Konsul trug man ein Beil voran,
Zu Rom, in alten Tagen.
Auch du hast deinen Liktor, doch wird
Das Beil dir nachgetragen.

»Ich bin dein Liktor, und ich geh
Beständig mit dem blanken
Richtbeile hinter dir – ich bin
Die Tat von deinem Gedanken.«


# VII


Ich ging nach Haus und schlief, als ob
Die Engel gewiegt mich hätten.
Man ruht in deutschen Betten so weich,
Denn das sind Federbetten.

Wie sehnt ich mich oft nach der Süßigkeit
Des vaterländischen Pfühles,
Wenn ich auf harten Matratzen lag,
In der schlaflosen Nacht des Exiles!

Man schläft sehr gut und träumt auch gut
In unseren Federbetten.
Hier fühlt die deutsche Seele sich frei
Von allen Erdenketten.

Sie fühlt sich frei und schwingt sich empor
Zu den höchsten Himmelsräumen.
O deutsche Seele, wie stolz ist dein Flug
In deinen nächtlichen Träumen!

'You are the judge, the bailiff I,
and like a retainer trusted
I execute the judgement you pass,
though it may be an injustice.

'In Rome they bore an axe before
the consul in procession.
You too have a lictor, but we've changed
the order of succession.

'I am your lictor, and I march
behind you, with axe well polished:
whenever your thought condemns a thing –
I act, and it's demolished.'


# VII


I went back home and slept as if
by angels serenaded.
You sleep so soft in German beds,
it's the feathers that they're made with.

How often through exile's sleepless night
I yearned for soft German bedding
and the sweetly restful pillow of home
to sink my weary head in.

There's no better place for sleep and dreams
than a German bed of feathers.
The German soul here feels itself free
of any earthly tethers.

It feels so free, it soars to touch
the heights of heaven eternal.
O German soul, how proud is your flight
during your dreams nocturnal!

Die Götter erbleichen, wenn du nahst!
Du hast auf deinen Wegen
Gar manches Sternlein ausgeputzt
Mit deinen Flügelschlägen!

Franzosen und Russen gehört das Land,
Das Meer gehört den Briten,
Wir aber besitzen im Luftreich des Traums
Die Herrschaft unbestritten.

Hier üben wir die Hegemonie,
Hier sind wir unzerstückelt;
Die andern Völker haben sich
Auf platter Erde entwickelt. – –

Und als ich einschlief, da träumte mir,
Ich schlenderte wieder im hellen
Mondschein die hallenden Straßen entlang,
In dem altertümlichen Cöllen.

Und hinter mir ging wieder einher
Mein schwarzer, vermummter Begleiter.
Ich war so müde, mir brachen die Knie,
Doch immer gingen wir weiter.

Wir gingen weiter. Mein Herz in der Brust
War klaffend aufgeschnitten,
Und aus der Herzenswunde hervor
Die roten Tropfen glitten.

Ich tauchte manchmal die Finger hinein,
Und manchmal ist es geschehen,
Daß ich die Haustürpfosten bestrich
Mit dem Blut im Vorübergehen.

Und jedesmal, wenn ich ein Haus
Bezeichnet in solcher Weise,
Ein Sterbeglöckchen erscholl fernher,
Wehmütig wimmernd und leise.

The gods grow pale at your approach,
your flight will take you far yet.
Already your wing-beat has snuffed out
more than one promising starlet.

The French and the Russians have shared out the land,
Britannia rules the oceans;
we reign unchallenged in the realm
of dreamy abstract notions.

Here we enjoy a hegemony,
for once we are not divided.
Other nations have kept their feet
on the ground with which they were provided.

When I fell asleep, I had a dream.
I was strolling again on my own
in the moonlight and the echoing streets
of the old part of Cologne.

My dark companion, with muffled face,
once more continued to tail me.
We kept on walking, on and on,
though my strength began to fail me.

We kept right on. My heart within
my breast was slit open wide,
I looked at the gaping wound and saw
the red drops glisten inside.

Sometimes I dipped my finger in,
and before the blood was dry
I'd paint a sign on the doorpost of
a house as we passed by.

And every time that thus I marked
a house with blood, the knell –
whimpering, melancholy, faint –
was rung by a distant bell.

Am Himmel aber erblich der Mond,
Er wurde immer trüber;
Gleich schwarzen Rossen jagten an ihm
Die wilden Wolken vorüber.

Und immer ging hinter mir einher
Mit seinem verborgenen Beile
Die dunkle Gestalt – so wanderten wir
Wohl eine gute Weile.

Wir gehen und gehen, bis wir zuletzt
Wieder zum Domplatz gelangen;
Weit offen standen die Pforten dort,
Wir sind hineingegangen.

Es herrschte im ungeheuren Raum
Nur Tod und Nacht und Schweigen;
Es brannten Ampeln hie und da,
Um die Dunkelheit recht zu zeigen.

Ich wandelte lange den Pfeilern entlang
Und hörte nur die Tritte
Von meinem Begleiter, er folgte mir
Auch hier bei jedem Schritte.

Wir kamen endlich zu einem Ort,
Wo funkelnde Kerzenhelle
Und blitzendes Gold und Edelstein;
Das war die Drei-Königs-Kapelle.

Die heilgen drei Könige jedoch,
Die sonst so still dort lagen,
O Wunder! sie saßen aufrecht jetzt
Auf ihren Sarkophagen.

Drei Totengerippe, phantastisch geputzt,
Mit Kronen auf den elenden
Vergilbten Schädeln, sie trugen auch
Das Zepter in knöchernen Händen.

And in the sky the moon grew pale,
her wan light ever receding;
across her face the wild clouds blew
like wild black horses stampeding.

And ever at my back there marched,
with his sinister instrument,
that muffled figure. So for a time
on through Cologne we went.

We walked and walked till at last we reached
the Cathedral Square once more,
straight into the Cathedral we went,
open wide was the door.

Death and night and silence reigned
in that enormous interior;
lights were burning here and there,
to make the darkness eerier.

Between the pillars I wandered long;
there was no sound but the pacing
of my relentless companion – here too
my every footstep tracing.

And finally we came to a place
where candlelight was sparkling;
gold was glinting and jewels shone,
while everywhere else was darkling.

The Three Kings' Chapel it was. But they
no longer lay unmoving.
Marvels! They now sat upright on
their carved sarcophagus roofing.

Skeletons three in fantastic garb,
with crowns upon their pathetic
yellowed skulls, and with sceptres clutched
in fingers bony, arthritic.

Wie Hampelmänner bewegten sie
Die längstverstorbenen Knochen;
Die haben nach Moder und zugleich
Nach Weihrauchduft gerochen.

Der Eine bewegte sogar den Mund
Und hielt eine Rede, sehr lange;
Er setzte mir auseinander, warum
Er meinen Respekt verlange.

Zuerst weil er ein Toter sei,
Und zweitens weil er ein König,
Und drittens weil er ein Heilger sei –
Das alles rührte mich wenig.

Ich gab ihm zur Antwort lachenden Muts:
Vergebens ist deine Bemühung!
Ich sehe, daß du der Vergangenheit
Gehörst in jeder Beziehung.

Fort! fort von hier! im tiefen Grab
Ist Eure natürliche Stelle.
Das Leben nimmt jetzt in Beschlag
Die Schätze dieser Kapelle.

Der Zukunft fröhliche Kavallerie
Soll hier im Dome hausen.
Und weicht Ihr nicht willig, so brauch ich Gewalt
Und laß Euch mit Kolben lausen!

So sprach ich, und ich drehte mich um,
Da sah ich furchtbar blinken
Des stummen Begleiters furchtbares Beil –
Und er verstand mein Winken.

Er nahte sich, und mit dem Beil
Zerschmetterte er die armen
Skelette des Aberglaubens, er schlug
Sie nieder ohn Erbarmen.

Their long-dead bones they slowly moved
like scarecrows, and they smelt too
of incense and, mixed in with that,
entombment's rot and mildew.

One of them even moved his mouth
and made a speech, a long one;
he explained why he thought my disrespect-
ful attitude the wrong one.

Firstly, the dead deserved respect,
next, kings might insist upon it,
and thirdly of course, he was a saint –
those were the bees in his bonnet.

I answered him with an easy laugh:
'You might as well stop trying.
I see you belong in all respects
to an age that's dead or dying.

'Take yourself off! The deepest grave
is the place for you and your kin there.
Life lays claim to your chapel now
and the treasures you've hoarded in there.

'The future's merry cavalry
shall camp in this sacred building;
if you don't go quietly, violence
will make you a bit more willing.'

Thus I spoke, and I turned about
and saw the terrible glinting
of my silent companion's terrible axe –
he knew what I was hinting.

Up he stepped and with one blow
the three poor skeletons shattered,
all the old bones of false beliefs
he mercilessly scattered.

Es dröhnte der Hiebe Widerhall
Aus allen Gewölben, entsetzlich, –
Blutströme schossen aus meiner Brust,
Und ich erwachte plötzlich.


## VIII

Von Cöllen bis Hagen kostet die Post
Fünf Taler sechs Groschen Preußisch.
Die Diligence war leider besetzt
Und ich kam in die offene Beichais.

Ein Spätherbstmorgen, feucht und grau,
Im Schlamme keuchte der Wagen;
Doch trotz des schlechten Wetters und Wegs
Durchströmte mich süßes Behagen.

Das ist ja meine Heimatluft!
Die glühende Wange empfand es!
Und dieser Landstraßenkot, er ist
Der Dreck meines Vaterlandes!

Die Pferde wedelten mit dem Schwanz
So traulich wie alte Bekannte,
Und ihre Mistküchlein dünkten mir schön
Wie die Äpfel der Atalante!

Wir fuhren durch Mühlheim. Die Stadt ist nett,
Die Menschen still und fleißig.
War dort zuletzt im Monat Mai
Das Jahres Einunddreißig.

Damals stand alles im Blütenschmuck
Und die Sonnenlichter lachten,
Die Vögel sangen sehnsuchtvoll,
Und die Menschen hofften und dachten –

High in the vaults his mighty blows
grimly reverberated.
Blood spurted from my breast – my dream
abruptly terminated.


## VIII

To get to Hagen from Cologne
costs five Prussian thaler six groschen.
The coach was full, so I had to ride
in the trailer, it wasn't a posh 'un.

A late autumn morning, damp and grey,
the coach-wheels ploughing mud;
bad weather, bad roads – but they couldn't damp
the contentment that pulsed in my blood.

I am breathing the air of home again!
My cheeks glow and understand.
And all this dirt on the road, it is
the filth of my fatherland.

Like a welcome from old acquaintances
were the waving tails of our dapples,
and their steaming dung seemed as beautiful
as Atalanta's apples.

We passed through Mühlheim. Nice little town,
the people quiet, hard-working.
The last time I was here was May
of AD one-and-thirty.

The splendour of blossom was everywhere then,
the sunlight was laughing and winking,
the birds were singing their courting songs
and people were hoping and thinking —

Sie dachten: »Die magere Ritterschaft
Wird bald von hinnen reisen,
Und der Abschiedstrunk wird ihnen kredenzt
Aus langen Flaschen von Eisen!

»Und die Freiheit kommt mit Spiel und Tanz,
Mit der Fahne, der weiß-blau-roten;
Vielleicht holt sie sogar aus dem Grab
Den Bonaparte, den Toten!«

Ach Gott! die Ritter sind immer noch hier,
Und manche dieser Gäuche,
Die spindeldürre gekommen ins Land,
Die haben jetzt dicke Bäuche.

Die blassen Kanaillen, die ausgesehn
Wie Liebe, Glauben und Hoffen,
Sie haben seitdem in unserm Wein
Sich rote Nasen gesoffen – – –

Und die Freiheit hat sich den Fuß verrenkt,
Kann nicht mehr springen und stürmen;
Die Trikolore in Paris
Schaut traurig herab von den Türmen.

Der Kaiser ist auferstanden seitdem,
Doch die englischen Würmer haben
Aus ihm einen stillen Mann gemacht,
Und er ließ sich wieder begraben.

Hab selber sein Leichenbegängnis gesehn,
Ich sah den goldenen Wagen
Und die goldenen Siegesgöttinnen drauf,
Die den goldenen Sarg getragen.

Den Elysäischen Feldern entlang,
Durch des Triumphes Bogen,
Wohl durch den Nebel, wohl über den Schnee
Kam langsam der Zug gezogen.

Thinking: 'The Scrawny Brotherhood
will soon have their bill to settle.
We'll offer them a farewell toast
from long thin tubes of metal!

'And freedom will come with dance and play
and bring the tricolour pennant;
perhaps she'll even bring back from the dead
the Corsican Lieutenant.'

But the Scrawny Brotherhood never went,
and many of their nation
who were thin as rakes when they came to these parts
now sport a corporation.

The pallid crew looked as full of fun
as the cardinal virtues in those days.
Since then they've learned to swill our wine
and make most days red-nose-days.

Freedom herself has sprained her foot
and lost her exuberant powers;
even in Paris the tricolour
looks sadly down from the towers.

The Emperor's been resurrected since,
but English worms had eaten
too much away. Now he's buried again –
he knew when he was beaten.

I was there myself at the ceremony:
gold victory goddesses holding
the golden coffin wherein he lay,
the coach itself was golden.

Along the Champs Elysées, to where
Old Triumph still stands arching,
on through the mist, on over the snow
the solemn procession came marching.

Mißtönend schauerlich war die Musik.
Die Musikanten starrten
Vor Kälte. Wehmütig grüßten mich
Die Adler der Standarten.

Die Menschen schauten so geisterhaft
In alter Erinnrung verloren –
Der imperiale Märchentraum
War wieder herauf beschworen.

Ich weinte an jenem Tag. Mir sind
Die Tränen ins Auge gekommen,
Als ich den verschollenen Liebesruf,
Das Vive l'Empereur! vernommen.


# IX

Von Cöllen war ich drei Viertel auf Acht
Des Morgens fortgereiset;
Wir kamen nach Hagen schon gegen Drei,
Da wird zu Mittag gespeiset.

Der Tisch war gedeckt. Hier fand ich ganz
Die altgermanische Küche.
Sei mir gegrüßt, mein Sauerkraut,
Holdselig sind deine Gerüche!

Gestovte Kastanien im grünen Kohl!
So aß ich sie einst bei der Mutter!
Ihr heimischen Stockfische, seid mir gegrüßt!
Wie schwimmt ihr klug in der Butter!

Jedwedem fühlenden Herzen bleibt
Das Vaterland ewig teuer –
Ich liebe auch recht braun geschmort
Die Bücklinge und Eier.

The music was grating, dissonant,
the musicians frozen-handed,
melancholy the greeting I had
from the eagle on every standard.

The people looked like ghosts that walked,
lost in old recollection –
the magic dream of empire had
a short, sad resurrection.

I wept that day. I could not keep
the tears in my eyes from welling,
to hear the lost cry of 'Vive l'Empereur!'
pathetically swelling.


# IX


It was quarter to eight when I left Cologne
that morning, as I've narrated.
We got to Hagen not much before three
for luncheon, somewhat belated.

They served up the real old Germanic food
from times near as ancient as Homer's.
Hail to thee, blithe sauerkraut,
delightful are thy aromas.

Boiled chestnuts mixed among the greens,
dear Mother, just like you did!
O cod of my homeland, you too I greet,
as you swim in that rich butter fluid!

Beats there a feeling heart, o say,
which holds not its fatherland sacred?
Personally, I'm also fond
of bloaters with eggs, well bakèd.

Wie jauchzten die Würste im spritzelnden Fett!
Die Krammetsvögel, die frommen
Gebratenen Englein mit Apfelmuß,
Sie zwitscherten mir: Willkommen!

Willkommen, Landsmann, – zwitscherten sie –
Bist lange ausgeblieben,
Hast dich mit fremdem Gevögel so lang
In der Fremde herumgetrieben!

Es stand auf dem Tische eine Gans,
Ein stilles, gemütliches Wesen.
Sie hat vielleicht mich einst geliebt,
Als wir beide noch jung gewesen.

Sie blickte mich an so bedeutungsvoll,
So innig, so treu, so wehe!
Besaß eine schöne Seele gewiß,
Doch war das Fleisch sehr zähe.

Auch einen Schweinskopf trug man auf
In einer zinnernen Schüssel;
Noch immer schmückt man den Schweinen bei uns
Mit Lorbeerblättern den Rüssel.


# X


Dicht hinter Hagen ward es Nacht,
Und ich fühlte in den Gedärmen
Ein seltsames Frösteln. Ich konnte mich erst
Zu Unna, im Wirtshaus, erwärmen.

Ein hübsches Mädchen fand ich dort,
Die schenkte mir freundlich den Punsch ein;
Wie gelbe Seide das Lockenhaar,
Die Augen sanft wie Mondschein.

How the sausages sang in the sizzling fat!
The fieldfares, little roast pious
angels served with apple sauce,
all twittered: 'Welcome! Do try us!

'Dear countryman, you've been long away,
now we're too pleased to see you for words.
You've been knocking about in foreign parts
all this time, with those foreign birds!'

A quiet homely German goose
was waiting to still my hunger.
Perhaps she loved me long ago
when both of us were younger.

She gave me a look so soulful, so true,
so meaning, with injured love's eyes.
I'm sure she had a beautiful soul,
but her flesh was a bit on the tough side.

They served us pig's head too. It says
a lot about German morals
that we stick to this quaint old custom. Our swine
still get decorated with laurels.


# X


Just after Hagen, night came down
and I felt in my intestines
a creeping cold. I couldn't get warm
till Unna, in one of its best inns.

I found a pretty maiden there,
her eyes were bright as stars; full
lovely the silken gold of her hair;
she also kept my glass full.

73

Den lispelnd westfälischen Akzent
Vernahm ich mit Wollust wieder.
Viel süße Erinnerung dampfte der Punsch,
Ich dachte der lieben Brüder,

Der lieben Westfalen, womit ich so oft
In Göttingen getrunken,
Bis wir gerührt einander ans Herz
Und unter die Tische gesunken!

Ich habe sie immer so lieb gehabt,
Die lieben, guten Westfalen,
Ein Volk so fest, so sicher, so treu,
Ganz ohne Gleißen und Prahlen.

Wie standen sie prächtig auf der Mensur
Mit ihren Löwenherzen!
Es fielen so grade, so ehrlich gemeint,
Die Quarten und die Terzen.

Sie fechten gut, sie trinken gut,
Und wenn sie die Hand dir reichen
Zum Freundschaftsbündnis, dann weinen sie;
Sind sentimentale Eichen.

Der Himmel erhalte dich, wackres Volk,
Er segne deine Saaten,
Bewahre dich vor Krieg und Ruhm,
Vor Helden und Heldentaten.

Er schenke deinen Söhnen stets
Ein sehr gelindes Examen,
Und deine Töchter bringe er hübsch
Unter die Haube – Amen!

As I heard that attractive Westphalian lisp,
I thought with pleasure of others.
The fumes of the punch brought back old times,
I thought of my dear, dear brothers,

Westphalians all – how often we'd drink
as much as we were able,
till we sank in each other's loving embrace
and slowly under the table.

I liked them so much in my Göttingen days,
those dear good lads of Westphalia.
They made no show, they put on no airs,
they were fellows who'd never fail you.

They were stalwarts at duelling, every one
in his breast a lion's heart carried.
They were all upstanding, sporting chaps,
as they honestly thrust and parried.

Their fencing and drinking is fine and fair,
their friendship has the same quality:
when they give you their hand on it, they weep,
hearts of oak, with some sentimentality.

May heaven guard you, doughty race,
and keep your crops richly bearing;
may it preserve you from wars and fame
and heroes and deeds of daring.

God grant your sons may pass their exams
without a fail or falter,
and may He bring your daughters all
safe and well-matched to the altar.

Das ist der Teutoburger Wald,
Den Tacitus beschrieben,
Das ist der klassische Morast,
Wo Varus stecken geblieben.

Hier schlug ihn der Cheruskerfürst,
Der Hermann, der edle Recke;
Die deutsche Nationalität,
Die siegte in diesem Drecke.

Wenn Hermann nicht die Schlacht gewann,
Mit seinen blonden Horden,
So gäb es deutsche Freiheit nicht mehr,
Wir wären römisch geworden!

In unserem Vaterland herrschten jetzt
Nur römische Sprache und Sitten,
Vestalen gäb es in München sogar,
Die Schwaben hießen Quiriten!

Der Hengstenberg wär ein Haruspex
Und grübelte in den Gedärmen
Von Ochsen. Neander wär ein Augur
Und schaute nach Vögelschwärmen.

Birch-Pfeiffer söffe Terpentin,
Wie einst die römischen Damen.
(Man sagt, daß sie dadurch den Urin
Besonders wohlriechend bekamen.)

Der Raumer wäre kein deutscher Lump,
Er wäre ein römscher Lumpacius.
Der Freiligrath dichtete ohne Reim,
Wie weiland Flaccus Horatius.

# XI

This is the forest of Teutoburg,
you probably know it from Tacitus.
This is where Varus got himself stuck,
the classic boggy morass it was.

The Cheruscan prince defeated him here,
Arminius, alias Hermann;
the German principle won the day,
the muck was also German.

Just think, if Arminius's blond horde
had lost to the foreign foeman,
would German liberty be what it is?
We should have all been Roman.

Rome's language and Rome's ways would reign,
there'd be vestal virgins in Munich,
those dear little Swabians would look so sweet
in Roman toga or tunic.

We'd have Hengstenberg as a haruspex,
over ox's offal pondering,
and Neander as augur on the watch
for flocks of wild birds wandering.

Birch-Pfeiffer'd be swigging turpentine,
like Rome's ladies aristocratic.
(It's said that a side effect was to make
their urine aromatic.)

Raumer would not be a German clod,
he'd be a Roman Clodius;
Freiligrath's poems would have no rhymes,
though they'd be no more melodious.

Der grobe Bettler, Vater Jahn,
Der hieße jetzt Grobianus.
Me hercule! Maßmann spräche Latein,
Der Marcus Tullius Maßmanus!

Die Wahrheitsfreunde würden jetzt
Mit Löwen, Hyänen, Schakalen
Sich raufen in der Arena, anstatt
Mit Hunden in kleinen Journalen.

Wir hätten Einen Nero jetzt
Statt Landesväter drei Dutzend.
Wir schnitten uns die Adern auf,
Den Schergen der Knechtschaft trutzend.

Der Schelling wär ganz ein Seneca,
Und käme in solchem Konflikt um.
Zu unsrem Cornelius sagten wir:
Cacatum non est pictum.

Gottlob! Der Hermann gewann die Schlacht,
Die Römer wurden vertrieben,
Varus mit seinen Legionen erlag,
Und wir sind Deutsche geblieben!

Wir blieben deutsch, wir sprechen deutsch,
Wie wir es gesprochen haben;
Der Esel heißt Esel, nicht asinus,
Die Schwaben blieben Schwaben.

Der Raumer blieb ein deutscher Lump
Und kriegt den Adlerorden.
In Reimen dichtet Freiligrath,
Ist kein Horaz geworden.

Gottlob, der Maßmann spricht kein Latein,
Birch-Pfeiffer schreibt nur Dramen
Und säuft nicht schnöden Terpentin
Wie Roms galante Damen.

There'd be a Latin name for Father
Jahn, that vulgar bully.
*Me Hercule*! Massmann would hold forth
in polished Latin like Tully.

Lovers of truth would have to fight
with jackals, lions and hyenas,
and not – as now – with dogs in trivial
journalistic arenas.

We'd have a single Nero now
instead of princes in dozens.
We'd slit a vein to escape his spite
like our noble Roman cousins.

Schelling would nobly take his life
in line with Seneca's dictum.
We'd look at Cornelius' pictures and say:
'*Cacatum non est pictum.*'

Thank God! The Romans were beaten then,
soundly enough to deter them.
Varus with all his legions was lost,
and Germany stayed German.

Germans we stayed, and Germans we are,
and German's the language we gas in –
a German says 'ass', not 'asinus'
(he has ways to be an ass in).

Raumer remained a German clod,
they even gave him a medal.
Freiligrath isn't a Horace, of course;
he just has his rhymes to peddle.

Massmann, praise be, knows no Latin at all,
Birch-Pfeiffer's penchant is dramatic,
she needn't tipple turpentine
to be aristo-aromatic.

O Hermann, dir verdanken wir das!
Drum wird dir, wie sich gebühret,
Zu Detmold ein Monument gesetzt;
Hab selber subskribieret.


## XII

Im nächtlichen Walde humpelt dahin
Die Chaise. Da kracht es plötzlich –
Ein Rad ging los. Wir halten still.
Das ist nicht sehr ergötzlich.

Der Postillon steigt ab und eilt
Ins Dorf, und ich verweile
Um Mitternacht allein im Wald.
Ringsum ertönt ein Geheule.

Das sind die Wölfe, die heulen so wild,
Mit ausgehungerten Stimmen.
Wie Lichter in der Dunkelheit
Die feurigen Augen glimmen.

Sie hörten von meiner Ankunft gewiß,
Die Bestien, und mir zu Ehre
Illuminierten sie den Wald
Und singen sie ihre Chöre.

Das ist ein Ständchen, ich merke es jetzt,
Ich soll gefeiert werden!
Ich warf mich gleich in Positur
Und sprach mit gerührten Gebärden:

»Mitwölfe! ich bin glücklich heut
In Eurer Mitte zu weilen,
Wo so viel edle Gemüter mir
Mit Liebe entgegenheulen.

O Hermann, for all this we've you to thank!
So at Detmold, as is fitting,
they're building you a monument –
I've even put my bit in.


# XII


It is night. Our chaise bumps on through the woods.
Suddenly there's a cracking –
a wheel's come off. We stop. All's still.
This is a bit nerve-racking.

Off the postilion goes – how far
will the nearest village or town be?
It's midnight. I am alone in the wood.
A howling starts up all around me.

That's the wolves, their howling is wild,
they sound as if they're ravenous.
I see their fiery eyes aglow
all round in the darkness cavernous.

It seems the news of my approach
has travelled on before us.
It's for me they've illuminated the wood,
and now they're singing a chorus.

It's a serenade. Ah! now I see,
they're treating me to the red carpet.
I strike a pose and make a speech,
with emotional gestures to mark it:

'Dear fellow wolves! To be in your midst
today makes me truly happy –
and to have so many noble minds
howling lovingly at me.

81

»Was ich in diesem Augenblick
Empfinde, ist unermeßlich;
Ach! diese schöne Stunde bleibt
Mir ewig unvergeßlich.

»Ich danke Euch für das Vertraun,
Womit Ihr mich beehret
Und das Ihr in jeder Prüfungszeit
Durch treue Beweise bewähret.

»Mitwölfe! Ihr zweifeltet nie an mir,
Ihr ließet Euch nicht fangen
Von Schelmen, die Euch gesagt, ich sei
Zu den Hunden übergegangen,

»Ich sei abtrünnig und werde bald
Hofrat in der Lämmerhürde –
Dergleichen zu widersprechen war
Ganz unter meiner Würde.

»Der Schafpelz, den ich umgehängt
Zuweilen, um mich zu wärmen,
Glaubt mirs, er brachte mich nie dahin,
Für das Glück der Schafe zu schwärmen.

»Ich bin kein Schaf, ich bin kein Hund,
Kein Hofrat und kein Schellfisch –
Ich bin ein Wolf geblieben, mein Herz
Und meine Zähne sind wölfisch.

»Ich bin ein Wolf und werde stets
Auch heulen mit den Wölfen –
Ja, zählt auf mich und helft Euch selbst,
Dann wird auch Gott Euch helfen!«

Das war die Rede, die ich hielt,
Ganz ohne Vorbereitung;
Verstümmelt hat Kolb sie abgedruckt
In der Allgemeinen Zeitung.

'The feelings that this moment inspires
are the kind that never perish.
Yes! This is one of the hours, I know,
that my heart will always cherish.

'I thank you for the trust which you
reposed in me. It was knowing
in testing times of your unfail-
ing support that kept me going.

'My friends! You never doubted me,
you never let rascals deceive you
who spread the tale that I was well in
with the dogs and planned to leave you,

'that I was a traitor, after high rank
among the Sheepish nation –
I didn't consider such rumours deserved
the honour of refutation.

'If ever I put sheep's clothing on,
it was purely a practical measure,
it kept me warm, but I never felt
that Sheepdom afforded much pleasure.

'I'm not a sheep, I'm not a dog,
not after high rank, not selfish –
I've always remained a wolf, my heart
and these teeth of mine are wolfish.

'A wolf – I shall always howl with you
from no more than a little distance.
So count on me and help yourselves,
the Lord will add his assistance.'

That was the speech I made – a speech
is always improvisable.
Kolb's *Allgemeine* printed it:
it was quite unrecognisable.

# XIII

Die Sonne ging auf bei Paderborn,
Mit sehr verdroßner Gebärde.
Sie treibt in der Tat ein verdrießlich Geschäft –
Beleuchten die dumme Erde!

Hat sie die eine Seite erhellt,
Und bringt sie mit strahlender Eile
Der andern ihr Licht, so verdunkelt schon
Sich jene mittlerweile.

Der Stein entrollt dem Sisyphus,
Der Danaiden Tonne
Wird nie gefüllt, und den Erdenball
Beleuchtet vergeblich die Sonne! –

Und als der Morgennebel zerrann,
Da sah ich am Wege ragen,
Im Frührotschein, das Bild des Manns,
Der an das Kreuz geschlagen.

Mit Wehmut erfüllt mich jedesmal
Dein Anblick, mein armer Vetter,
Der du die Welt erlösen gewollt,
Du Narr, du Menschheitsretter!

Sie haben dir übel mitgespielt,
Die Herren vom hohen Rate.
Wer hieß dich auch reden so rücksichtslos
Von der Kirche und vom Staate!

Zu deinem Malheur war die Buchdruckerei
Noch nicht in jenen Tagen
Erfunden; du hättest geschrieben ein Buch
Über die Himmelsfragen.

# XIII

The sun came up near Paderborn
as if he was bored and weary.
The job of lighting the stupid earth
is understandably dreary.

He's only just lit one side up
and is hastening round to the other,
when his light already fades on the first,
and the powers of darkness recover.

Sisyphus' stone rolls down again,
the Danaids' cask can never
be filled, and the sun will go on in vain
lighting the earth for ever!

And when the early mists had cleared
I saw in the light of morning
a roadside image of the man
they nailed on the cross as a warning.

Poor cousin, it always makes me sad
when I recall your behaviour;
you wanted to redeem the world,
you fool, to play the saviour!

They played a nasty trick on you,
those high Establishment Pharisees.
Criticism of Church and State
was the worst of all possible heresies.

If only you'd written a *book* to show
that religion needed renewing.
But printing wasn't invented then,
that was your undoing.

Der Zensor hätte gestrichen darin
Was etwa anzüglich auf Erden,
Und liebend bewahrte dich die Zensur
Vor dem Gekreuzigtwerden.

Ach! hättest du nur einen andern Text
Zu deiner Bergpredigt genommen,
Besaßest ja Geist und Talent genug,
Und konntest schonen die Frommen!

Geldwechsler, Bankiers, hast du sogar
Mit der Peitsche gejagt aus dem Tempel –
Unglücklicher Schwärmer, jetzt hängst du am Kreuz
Als warnendes Exempel!


## XIV


Ein feuchter Wind, ein kahles Land,
Die Chaise wackelt im Schlamme,
Doch singt es und klingt es in meinem Gemüt:
Sonne, du klagende Flamme!

Das ist der Schlußreim des alten Lieds,
Das oft meine Amme gesungen –
»Sonne, du klagende Flamme!« das hat
Wie Waldhornruf geklungen.

Es kommt im Lied ein Mörder vor,
Der lebt' in Lust und Freude;
Man findet ihn endlich im Walde gehenkt,
An einer grauen Weide.

Des Mörders Todesurteil war
Genagelt am Weidenstamme;
Das haben die Rächer der Feme getan –
Sonne, du klagende Flamme!

The censor would have cut what fell
in his worldly jurisdiction;
Censorship would have lovingly
preserved you from crucifixion.

If only your Sermon on the Mount
had shown no political bias –
you had talent and intellect enough
not to tread on the corns of the pious.

You even whipped from the temple courts
the bankers and money-changers –
hapless idealist, there you now hang
to warn us ideals have dangers.


## XIV


A raw wind and a barren land,
the chaise is bogged in the mire,
but my mind is singing with ringing words:
'Sun, thou accusing fire.'

That's the last line of the ancient song
my nurse would sing in my childhood –
'Sun, thou accusing fire!' – like a horn
ringing through the wild wood.

The song tells of a murderer
who lay on fortune's soft pillow.
But at the end he's found in a wood,
hanged from a grey willow.

There on the willow trunk was nailed
the murderer's sentence dire;
the secret avengers had caught him up –
'Sun, thou accusing fire.'

Die Sonne war Kläger, sie hatte bewirkt,
Daß man den Mörder verdamme.
Ottilie hatte sterbend geschrien:
Sonne, du klagende Flamme!

Und denk ich des Liedes, so denk ich auch
Der Amme, der lieben Alten;
Ich sehe wieder ihr braunes Gesicht,
Mit allen Runzeln und Falten.

Sie war geboren im Münsterland,
Und wußte, in großer Menge,
Gespenstergeschichten, grausenhaft,
Und Märchen und Volksgesänge.

Wie pochte mein Herz, wenn die alte Frau
Von der Königstochter erzählte,
Die einsam auf der Heide saß
Und die goldnen Haare strählte.

Die Gänse mußte sie hüten dort
Als Gänsemagd, und trieb sie
Am Abend die Gänse wieder durchs Tor,
Gar traurig stehen blieb sie.

Denn angenagelt über dem Tor
Sah sie ein Roßhaupt ragen,
Das war der Kopf des armen Pferds,
Das sie in die Fremde getragen.

Die Königstochter seufzte tief:
O, Falada, daß du hangest!
Der Pferdekopf herunter rief:
O wehe! daß du gangest!

Die Königstochter seufzte tief:
Wenn das meine Mutter wüßte!
Der Pferdekopf herunter rief:
Ihr Herze brechen müßte!

The sun's rays had accused him first
the sentence of death to require.
The murdered maiden's dying appeal
was 'Sun, thou accusing fire!'

When I think of that tale, I also think
of my dear old nurse who told it;
I see again her old brown face,
the skin all wrinkled and folded.

She was born in the heart of the Münsterland
and knew innumerable
ghostly stories to chill your spine,
fairy-tale, folk-song and fable.

How my heart would thump when she told the tale
of that loneliest of princesses,
who sat in the middle of the heath
combing her golden tresses.

They set her there to mind the geese,
and when at nightfall returning
the goosegirl drove them back into town
she was filled with sadness and yearning.

For nailed up high above the gate
was the head of a horse on the tower,
the luckless horse that bore her off
into the strangers' power.

Deeply the royal princess sighed:
'Alas! that you hang there so!'
The horse's head cried down to her:
'Alas! that you pass there below!'

The royal princess sighed so deep:
'If only my mother knew it!'
The horse's head cried down to her:
'Her heart would sorely rue it.'

Mit stockendem Atem horchte ich hin,
Wenn die Alte ernster und leiser
Zu sprechen begann und vom Rotbart sprach,
Von unserem heimlichen Kaiser.

Sie hat mir versichert, er sei nicht tot,
Wie da glauben die Gelehrten,
Er hause versteckt in einem Berg
Mit seinen Waffengefährten.

Kyffhäuser ist der Berg genannt,
Und drinnen ist eine Höhle;
Die Ampeln erhellen so geisterhaft
Die hochgewölbten Säle.

Ein Marstall ist der erste Saal,
Und dorten kann man sehen
Viel tausend Pferde, blankgeschirrt,
Die an den Krippen stehen.

Sie sind gesattelt und gezäumt,
Jedoch von diesen Rossen
Kein einziges wiehert, kein einziges stampft,
Sind still, wie aus Eisen gegossen.

Im zweiten Saale, auf der Streu,
Sieht man Soldaten liegen,
Viel tausend Soldaten, bärtiges Volk,
Mit kriegerisch trotzigen Zügen.

Sie sind gerüstet von Kopf bis Fuß,
Doch alle diese Braven,
Sie rühren sich nicht, bewegen sich nicht,
Sie liegen fest und schlafen.

Hochaufgestapelt im dritten Saal
Sind Schwerter, Streitäxte, Speere,
Harnische, Helme, von Silber und Stahl,
Altfränkische Feuergewehre.

With bated breath I listened when
my nurse grew grave and confiding,
her hushed voice spoke the Red-Beard's name,
our Emperor-in-hiding.

She assured me that he wasn't dead,
as the learned gentlemen tell us,
but hiding deep in a mountain's heart
with all his well-armed fellows.

Kyffhäuser is the mountain's name
and a cave is at its centre.
Ghostly gleams illumine the halls,
the light of day cannot enter.

The first hall is a stable vast;
the astonished eye there ranges
o'er thousands of horses, harness bright,
standing at their mangers.

All are bridled and saddled up,
all are in perfect fettle,
yet none ever whinnies or paws the ground.
They stand as if cast in metal.

In the second hall, upon the straw,
you see the soldiers lying,
thousands on thousands, bearded men,
warlike and death-defying,

all of them armed from top to toe,
the Emperor's ancient might;
but they do not move a muscle, they lie
and sleep through the long night.

In the hall beyond lie swords and spears
and axes ready for taking,
armour and helmets of silver and steel,
and fire-arms of antique making.

Sehr wenig Kanonen, jedoch genug
Um eine Trophäe zu bilden.
Hoch ragt daraus eine Fahne hervor,
Die Farbe ist schwarz-rot-gülden.

Der Kaiser bewohnt den vierten Saal.
Schon seit Jahrhunderten sitzt er
Auf steinernem Stuhl, am steinernen Tisch,
Das Haupt auf den Armen stützt er.

Sein Bart, der bis zur Erde wuchs,
Ist rot wie Feuerflammen,
Zuweilen zwinkert er mit dem Aug,
Zieht manchmal die Braunen zusammen.

Schläft er oder denkt er nach?
Man kanns nicht genau ermitteln;
Doch wenn die rechte Stunde kommt,
Wird er gewaltig sich rütteln.

Die gute Fahne ergreift er dann
Und ruft: zu Pferd! zu Pferde!
Sein reisiges Volk erwacht und springt
Lautrasselnd empor von der Erde.

Ein jeder schwingt sich auf sein Roß,
Das wiehert und stampft mit den Hufen!
Sie reiten hinaus in die klirrende Welt,
Und die Trompeten rufen.

Sie reiten gut, sie schlagen gut,
Sie haben ausgeschlafen.
Der Kaiser hält ein strenges Gericht,
Er will die Mörder bestrafen —

Die Mörder, die gemeuchelt einst
Die teure, wundersame,
Goldlockigte Jungfrau Germania —
Sonne, du klagende Flamme!

Not many cannon, but enough
to make a trophy of them.
A standard too, in red-black-gold,
proudly rises above them.

In the furthest hall, the Emperor sits
just as centuries have seen him –
at a table of stone, on a chair of stone,
arms propped, his head between them.

The beard that grows right down to his feet
is vivid red like fire.
From time to time he twitches a lid,
or raises one eyebrow higher.

Is he asleep, or does he brood?
It is easy to be mistaken.
But when the fated hour comes,
he will rise with a mighty shaking.

He will seize the good flag in his hand
and cry: 'To horse!' and 'Forward!'
His men will awake and clanking rise
from the earth to follow their warlord.

Into the saddle they swing, their steeds
are whinnying now and pawing,
they ride out into a clattering world
with all the trumpets calling.

They will ride like men, they will fight like men,
after their long, deep slumber.
The Emperor will sit in judgment stern
on all that murderous number —

murderers who to do to death
a maiden did once conspire,
my wondrous golden-haired Germany –
'Sun, thou accusing fire!'

Wohl mancher, der sich geborgen geglaubt,
Und lachend auf seinem Schloß saß,
Er wird nicht entgehen dem rächenden Strang,
Dem Zorne Barbarossas! – – –

Wie klingen sie lieblich, wie klingen sie süß,
Die Märchen der alten Amme!
Mein abergläubisches Herze jauchzt:
Sonne, du klagende Flamme!


## XV


Ein feiner Regen prickelt herab,
Eiskalt, wie Nähnadelspitzen.
Die Pferde bewegen traurig den Schwanz,
Sie waten im Kot und schwitzen.

Der Postillon stößt in sein Horn,
Ich kenne das alte Getute –
»Es reiten drei Reiter zum Tor hinaus!« –
Es wird mir so dämmrig zu Mute.

Mich schläferte und ich entschlief,
Und siehe! mir träumte am Ende,
Daß ich mich in dem Wunderberg
Beim Kaiser Rotbart befände.

Er saß nicht mehr auf steinernem Stuhl,
Am steinernen Tisch, wie ein Steinbild;
Auch sah er nicht so ehrwürdig aus,
Wie man sich gewöhnlich einbildt.

Er watschelte durch die Säle herum
Mit mir im trauten Geschwätze.
Er zeigte wie ein Antiquar
Mir seine Kuriosa und Schätze.

There's many a castle feels solid and safe
to its laughing, complacent lord,
yet he won't escape the Emperor's wrath
or the Emperor's avenging cord.

How lovely they sound, how sweet they sound,
those songs from the people's lyre!
My superstitious heart exults:
'Sun, thou accusing fire!'


# XV


A fine rain is falling, its needle points
prick us and freeze the blood;
the horses sadly twitch their tails
and sweat as they wade through the mud.

The postilion blows a tune on his horn,
I know the good old rouser –
'Three horsemen went riding out through the gate' –
I feel myself getting drowsier.

The motion rocks me and off I nod,
and behold! a dream translates me
into that wondrous mountain-cave
where Barbarossa awaits me.

No more on a stony seat he sat,
at a table of stone, like a statue,
nor did he have that imposing air
with which great men look at you.

He waddled about in those halls with me,
our talk was quite familiar;
he showed me his collection of arms
and other memorabilia.

Im Saale der Waffen erklärte er mir,
Wie man sich der Kolben bediene,
Von einigen Schwertern rieb er den Rost
Mit seinem Hermeline.

Er nahm ein Pfauenwedel zur Hand,
Und reinigte vom Staube
Gar manchen Harnisch, gar manchen Helm,
Auch manche Pickelhaube.

Die Fahne stäubte er gleichfalls ab,
Und er sprach: »Mein größter Stolz ist,
Daß noch keine Motte die Seide zerfraß,
Und auch kein Wurm im Holz ist.«

Und als wir kamen in den Saal,
Wo schlafend am Boden liegen
Viel tausend Krieger, kampfbereit,
Der Alte sprach mit Vergnügen:

»Hier müssen wir leiser reden und gehn,
Damit wir nicht wecken die Leute;
Wieder verflossen sind hundert Jahr,
Und Löhnungstag ist heute.«

Und siehe! der Kaiser nahte sich sacht
Den schlafenden Soldaten,
Und steckte heimlich in die Tasch
Jedwedem einen Dukaten.

Er sprach mit schmunzelndem Gesicht,
Als ich ihn ansah verwundert:
»Ich zahle einen Dukaten per Mann,
Als Sold, nach jedem Jahrhundert.«

Im Saale, wo die Pferde stehn
In langen, schweigenden Reihen,
Da rieb der Kaiser sich die Händ,
Schien sonderbar sich zu freuen.

He showed me what a handy thing
for tight corners an old-fashioned mace is.
He polished some swords with his ermine robe,
there was rust in one or two places.

The helmets and armour were thick with dust,
so he took a feather duster
and flicked it off. Some headgear with spikes
likewise had to pass muster.

He also shook out the dust from his flag,
and said: 'Now this is good work –
we've kept the moths from eating the silk,
and the woodworm out of the woodwork.'

And when we presently entered the hall,
where as far as the eye could measure
fully-armed warriors lay asleep,
the old man said with pleasure:

'We'll have to keep quiet, and not interrupt
the slumber you see my chaps in;
today is payday, a hundred years
are once more on the point of elapsing.'

And behold! as we passed each sleeping man,
the Emperor took a ducat,
crept gently up to the warrior's side
and slipped it into his pocket.

Then he said to me, with a grin on his face,
as I looked at him in amazement:
'A ducat apiece per hundred years,
those are their terms of engagement.'

In the next hall, where in silent rows
stood all the Emperor's horses,
he rubbed his hands, and seemed well pleased
at the sight of his equine resources.

Er zählte die Gäule, Stück vor Stück,
Und klätschelte ihnen die Rippen;
Er zählte und zählte, mit ängstlicher Hast
Bewegten sich seine Lippen.

»Das ist noch nicht die rechte Zahl« –
Sprach er zuletzt verdrossen –
»Soldaten und Waffen hab ich genung,
Doch fehlt es noch an Rossen.

»Roßkämme habe ich ausgeschickt
In alle Welt, die kaufen
Für mich die besten Pferde ein,
Hab schon einen guten Haufen.

»Ich warte, bis die Zahl komplett,
Dann schlag ich los und befreie
Mein Vaterland, mein deutsches Volk,
Das meiner harret mit Treue.«

So sprach der Kaiser, ich aber rief:
Schlag los, du alter Geselle,
Schlag los, und hast du nicht Pferde genug,
Nimm Esel an ihrer Stelle.

Der Rotbart erwiderte lächelnd: »Es hat
Mit dem Schlagen gar keine Eile,
Man baute nicht Rom in einem Tag,
Gut Ding will haben Weile.

»Wer heute nicht kommt, kommt morgen gewiß,
Nur langsam wächst die Eiche,
Und chi va piano va sano, so heißt
Das Sprüchwort im römischen Reiche.«

He counted the horses one by one
and patted their flanks with affection;
I saw his lips move with anxious haste
as he counted them, section by section.

'They still aren't up to strength,' he said
at last, in some irritation;
'I've plenty of soldiers and plenty of arms,
but I'm short of transportation.

'We need more mounts – I've sent out men
in all directions to get 'em,
none but the best. You see we've a lot,
though we've not reached the target I set 'em.

'But when there's enough, I'll strike and put
my plans into operation.
My fatherland, my faithful folk
are longing for liberation.'

Thus spoke the Emperor, but I cried:
'Why wait? It'll serve no purpose.
Strike now, old fellow. If horses are short,
then even an ass will do service.'

Then Barbarossa smiled and replied:
'There's time to wait till we're ready.
Rome wasn't built in a day – if a job's
worth doing, it's worth taking steady.

'Tomorrow's another day, more haste
less speed, *festina lente*
and *chi va piano va sano* – you see,
there's wisdom in proverbs aplenty.'

# XVI

Das Stoßen des Wagens weckte mich auf,
Doch sanken die Augenlider
Bald wieder zu, und ich entschlief
Und träumte vom Rotbart wieder.

Ging wieder schwatzend mit ihm herum
Durch alle die hallenden Säle;
Er frug mich dies, er frug mich das,
Verlangte, daß ich erzähle.

Er hatte aus der Oberwelt
Seit vielen, vielen Jahren,
Wohl seit dem siebenjährigen Krieg,
Kein Sterbenswort erfahren.

Er frug nach Moses Mendelssohn,
Nach der Karschin, mit Intresse
Frug er nach der Gräfin Dubarry,
Des fünfzehnten Ludwigs Mätresse.

O Kaiser, rief ich, wie bist du zurück!
Der Moses ist längst gestorben,
Nebst seiner Rebekka, auch Abraham,
Der Sohn, ist gestorben, verdorben.

Der Abraham hatte mit Lea erzeugt
Ein Bübchen, Felix heißt er,
Der brachte es weit im Christentum,
Ist schon Kapellenmeister.

Die alte Karschin ist gleichfalls tot,
Auch die Tochter ist tot, die Klenke;
Helmine Chézy, die Enkelin,
Ist noch am Leben, ich denke.

100

# XVI

The coach's jolting woke me up,
but soon my eyelids droop again
and I'm back in my dream with the Emperor
and all his ancient troop again.

We're chatting away again as we walk,
our steps keep the echoes stirring;
he's asking the questions now, I have
to tell him what's been occurring.

It's years and years since a scrap of news
from topsides filtered through to him;
since the Seven Years' War his source has dried up,
all that I say is new to him.

Moses Mendelssohn, Madame Karschin
were the objects of his enquiry;
when he asked after Madame Dubarry, then
his interest grew quite fiery.

'O Emperor,' I said, 'you're a bit behind,
'old Moses has long since passed on,
with Rebecca his wife – and Abraham
their son too is dead and gone.

'Abraham and Lea begat
a wee lad, Felix his name is;
he's made it among the Christians, as
an orchestral conductor, quite famous.

'Old Madame Karschin is dead as well,
and so's Madame Klencke, her daughter;
Helmine Chézy, her grandchild, though
has not yet passed over the water.

Die Dubarry lebte lustig und flott,
Solange Ludwig regierte,
Der Fünfzehnte nämlich, sie war schon alt,
Als man sie guillotinierte.


Der König Ludwig der Fünfzehnte starb
Ganz ruhig in seinem Bette,
Der Sechzehnte aber ward guillotiniert
Mit der Königin Antoinette.


Die Königin zeigte großen Mut,
Ganz wie es sich gebührte,
Die Dubarry aber weinte und schrie,
Als man sie guillotinierte. – –


Der Kaiser blieb plötzlich stille stehn,
Und sah mich an mit den stieren
Augen und sprach: »Um Gotteswilln,
Was ist das, guillotinieren?«


Das Guillotinieren – erklärte ich ihm –
Ist eine neue Methode,
Womit man die Leute jeglichen Stands
Vom Leben bringt zu Tode.


Bei dieser Methode bedient man sich
Auch einer neuen Maschine,
Die hat erfunden Herr Guillotin,
Drum nennt man sie Guillotine.


Du wirst hier an ein Brett geschnallt; –
Das senkt sich; – du wirst geschoben
Geschwinde zwischen zwei Pfosten; – es hängt
Ein dreieckig Beil ganz oben; –


Man zieht eine Schnur, dann schießt herab
Das Beil, ganz lustig und munter; –
Bei dieser Gelegenheit fällt dein Kopf
In einen Sack hinunter.

'Madame Dubarry lived it up
while Louis was a friend to her –
I mean the Fifteenth, she was getting on
when the guillotine put an end to her.

'Louis the Fifteenth died in bed,
but after him the flood began;
they guillotined the Sixteenth and his Queen
when the terrible reign of blood began.

'She bore herself nobly, Marie Antoinette,
Louis the Sixteenth's Queen,
But Madame Dubarry screamed and wept
when put under the guillotine.'

The Emperor suddenly stopped in his tracks
and stared at me with gleaming
eyes and said: 'For heaven's sake,
what is this guillotining?'

'The guillotine' – I explained to him –
'Is a recent innovation
for putting human beings to death
regardless of social station.

'The new procedure involves the use
of a certain new machine
invented by Monsieur Guillotin –
hence the name Guillotine.

'You're strapped down to a board, like so,
they lower it and shove you
promptly between two posts; a trian-
gular axe is hanging above you;

'They pull a string, the axe shoots down –
rather a jolly spectacle;
in the course of these proceedings, your head
falls into a waiting receptacle.'

Der Kaiser fiel mir in die Red:
»Schweig still, von deiner Maschine
Will ich nichts wissen, Gott bewahr,
Daß ich mich ihrer bediene!

»Der König und die Königin!
Geschnallt! an einem Brette!
Das ist ja gegen allen Respekt
Und alle Etikette!

»Und du, wer bist du, daß du es wagst,
Mich so vertraulich zu duzen?
Warte, du Bürschchen, ich werde dir schon
Die kecken Flügel stutzen!

»Es regt mir die innerste Galle auf,
Wenn ich dich höre sprechen,
Dein Odem schon ist Hochverrat
Und Majestätsverbrechen!«

Als solchermaßen in Eifer geriet
Der Alte und sonder Schranken
Und Schonung mich anschnob, da platzten heraus
Auch mir die geheimsten Gedanken.

Herr Rotbart – rief ich laut – du bist
Ein altes Fabelwesen,
Geh, leg dich schlafen, wir werden uns
Auch ohne dich erlösen.

Die Republikaner lachen uns aus,
Sehn sie an unserer Spitze
So ein Gespenst mit Zepter und Kron;
Sie rissen schlechte Witze.

Auch deine Fahne gefällt mir nicht mehr,
Die altdeutschen Narren verdarben
Mir schon in der Burschenschaft die Lust
An den schwarz-rot-goldnen Farben.

At this point the Emperor broke in:
'Be silent, I want no more news of it!
A horrid machine, the Lord forbid
that ever I should make use of it.

'The Sovereign and his Lady Queen!
Strapped down! It's a disgrace, sir!
Against all the rules of etiquette!
People should know their place, sir!

'And who d'you think you are to dare
converse with me like an equal?
Just wait, my lad, I'll take you down
a peg or two in the sequel!

'To hear you talk is quite enough
to goad me beyond reason.
You're guilty, I say, of lèse-majesté,
your very breath is treason!'

When the old man got so worked up
and lost all sense of proportion,
I started to speak my mind as well,
I threw away all caution.

'Barbarossa' – I cried in return –
'You're only some old fable,
go back to bed, we'll free ourselves
without you, we're quite able.

'If they were to see us led by a ghost
with sceptre and crown imperial,
the Republicans would laugh us to scorn,
we'd just be joke-material.

'And I don't much like your flag – I lost
my taste for the German Olden
Tymes when my fellow-students made
a fetish of black-red-golden.

Das beste wäre, du bliebest zu Haus,
Hier in dem alten Kyffhäuser –
Bedenk ich die Sache ganz genau,
So brauchen wir gar keinen Kaiser.


## XVII

Ich habe mich mit dem Kaiser gezankt
Im Traum, im Traum versteht sich, –
Im wachenden Zustand sprechen wir nicht
Mit Fürsten so widersetzig.

Nur träumend, im idealen Traum,
Wagt ihnen der Deutsche zu sagen
Die deutsche Meinung, die er so tief
Im treuen Herzen getragen.

Als ich erwacht', fuhr ich einem Wald
Vorbei, der Anblick der Bäume,
Der nackten hölzernen Wirklichkeit,
Verscheuchte meine Träume.

Die Eichen schüttelten ernsthaft das Haupt,
Die Birken und Birkenreiser
Sie nickten so warnend – und ich rief:
Vergib mir, mein teurer Kaiser!

Vergib mir, o Rotbart, das rasche Wort!
Ich weiß, du bist viel weiser
Als ich, ich habe so wenig Geduld –
Doch komme du bald, mein Kaiser!

Behagt dir das Guillotinieren nicht,
So bleib bei den alten Mitteln:
Das Schwert für Edelleute, der Strick
Für Bürger und Bauern in Kitteln.

'Perhaps on reflection you'd better stay
in your cave, a historical oddity;
for our present purposes, Emperors aren't
a necessary commodity.'


# XVII


I rowed with the Emperor in my dream –
in dream, please note my insistence;
faced with princes in waking hours,
we put up no such resistance.

It's only in the Utopia of dreams
that a German dare fling in their faces
the German opinion which he conceals
in his loyal heart's inmost places.

My dreams were finally chased away
by what I saw on waking –
the trees in a wood we were driving by,
wooden, and real, and naked.

The oak trees earnestly shook their heads,
I could feel their attitude harden.
Each birch tree, each twiglet nodded reproof,
and I cried 'Dear Emperor, pardon!

'Forgive, Barbarossa, my hasty word!
I know that you're so much wiser
than me, I'm not the patient sort –
but oh, how long, my Kaiser?

'If you don't much like the guillotine,
the good old method passes:
the sword for noblemen, the cord
for the burgher- and peasant-classes.

Nur manchmal wechsle ab, und laß
Den Adel hängen, und köpfe
Ein bißchen die Bürger und Bauern, wir sind
Ja alle Gottesgeschöpfe.

Stell wieder her das Halsgericht,
Das peinliche Karls des Fünften,
Und teile wieder ein das Volk
Nach Ständen, Gilden und Zünften.

Das alte heilige römische Reich,
Stells wieder her, das ganze,
Gib uns den modrigsten Plunder zurück
Mit allem Firlifanze.

Das Mittelalter, immerhin,
Das wahre, wie es gewesen,
Ich will es ertragen – erlöse uns nur
Von jenem Zwitterwesen,

Von jenem Kamaschenrittertum,
Das ekelhaft ein Gemisch ist
Von gotischem Wahn und modernem Lug,
Das weder Fleisch noch Fisch ist.

Jag fort das Komödiantenpack,
Und schließe die Schauspielhäuser,
Wo man die Vorzeit parodiert –
Komme du bald, o Kaiser!


XVIII


Minden ist eine feste Burg,
Hat gute Wehr und Waffen!
Mit preußischen Festungen hab ich jedoch
Nicht gerne was zu schaffen.

'But do hang a nobleman now and then,
and behead a burgher or peasant –
we're all God's children, after all,
and a change is always pleasant.

'Bring back the Lawcourts of Charles the Fifth,
that repressed the Reformation,
divide the people into estates,
into guild and corporation.

'The Holy Roman Empire of old,
yes, bring it back, lock, stock and barrel,
with all its musty junk and all
its trimming and fancy apparel.

'The Middle Ages, well, I suppose
if you give us the genuine article,
I'll put up with that. Just rescue us
from all this hybrid, farcical,

'revolting, pseudo-knightliness
which, under its Gothic cover,
is just a lot of modern deceit,
neither one thing nor the other.

'Throw out that pack of comedians
who parody times long gone,
and shut down their theatres once for all –
how long, o Emperor, how long?'


# XVIII


A mighty fortress is Minden town,
armed to the teeth, most alarming.
A stay in a Prussian stronghold's a thing
I find distinctly uncharming.

Wir kamen dort an zur Abendzeit.
Die Planken der Zugbrück stöhnten
So schaurig, als wir hinübergerollt;
Die dunklen Gräben gähnten.

Die hohen Bastionen schauten mich an,
So drohend und verdrossen;
Das große Tor ging rasselnd auf,
Ward rasselnd wieder geschlossen.

Ach! meine Seele ward betrübt,
Wie des Odysseus Seele,
Als er gehört, daß Polyphem
Den Felsblock schob vor die Höhle.

Es trat an den Wagen ein Korporal
Und frug uns: wie wir hießen?
Ich heiße Niemand, bin Augenarzt
Und steche den Star den Riesen.

Im Wirtshaus ward mir noch schlimmer zu Mut,
Das Essen wollt mir nicht schmecken.
Ging schlafen sogleich, doch schlief ich nicht,
Mich drückten so schwer die Decken.

Es war ein breites Federbett,
Gardinen von rotem Damaste,
Der Himmel von verblichenem Gold,
Mit einem schmutzigen Quaste.

Verfluchter Quast! der die ganze Nacht
Die liebe Ruhe mir raubte!
Er hing mir, wie des Damokles Schwert,
So drohend über dem Haupte!

Schien manchmal ein Schlangenkopf zu sein,
Und ich hörte ihn heimlich zischen:
Du bist und bleibst in der Festung jetzt,
Du kannst nicht mehr entwischen!

110

It was evening there when we arrived;
the drawbridge planks, to greet us,
groaned chillingly as we rolled across,
the dark moat yawned beneath us.

Tall bastions with threatening mien
looked down at me in anger;
the gate was opened with rattle of chains
and shut with equal clangour.

My heart sank at the sound, as once
in that cave the heart of Odysseus,
when he knew that Polyphemus's rock
had blocked the only issue.

Up to the coach stepped a corporal
to ask the name of his clients.
'My name is Noman, oculist,
and I let light into giants.'

I felt even worse when we got to the inn,
even the meal was no pleasure.
I went straight to bed, but I couldn't sleep
for the bedclothes' uncomfortable pressure.

It was a good wide feather-bed,
it had red damask curtains,
the canopy was faded gold,
with a tassel, rather dirty.

That bloody tassel! All night long
my beauty-sleep it wrought havoc with,
hung threatening above my head
just like the sword of Damocles.

Sometimes it seemed the head of a snake,
and I heard its sinister sibilance:
'You're in the fortress, and here you'll stay,
you won't escape our vigilance.'

O, daß ich wäre – seufzte ich –
Daß ich zu Hause wäre,
Bei meiner lieben Frau in Paris,
Im Faubourg-Poissonnière!

Ich fühlte, wie über die Stirne mir
Auch manchmal etwas gestrichen,
Gleich einer kalten Zensorhand,
Und meine Gedanken wichen –

Gendarmen in Leichenlaken gehüllt,
Ein weißes Spukgewirre,
Umringte mein Bett, ich hörte auch
Unheimliches Kettengeklirre.

Ach! die Gespenster schleppten mich fort
Und ich hab mich endlich befunden
An einer steilen Felsenwand;
Dort war ich festgebunden.

Der böse schmutzige Betthimmelquast!
Ich fand ihn gleichfalls wieder,
Doch sah er jetzt wie ein Geier aus,
Mit Krallen und schwarzem Gefieder.

Er glich dem preußischen Adler jetzt,
Und hielt meinen Leib umklammert;
Er fraß mir die Leber aus der Brust,
Ich habe gestöhnt und gejammert.

Ich jammerte lange – da krähte der Hahn,
Und der Fiebertraum erblaßte.
Ich lag zu Minden im schwitzenden Bett,
Der Adler ward wieder zum Quaste.

Ich reiste fort mit Extrapost,
Und schöpfte freien Odem
Erst draußen in der freien Natur,
Auf bückeburgschem Boden.

'Oh dear' – I sighed – 'I wish I was back
in the Faubourg Poissonnière
in Paris, with my dearest wife,
enjoying her loving care!'

And sometimes something brushed across
my forehead, I felt it on me
just like an icy censor's hand –
my thoughts all vanished promptly.

Gendarmes wrapped in winding sheets
kept my bed surrounded,
a white confusion of spooks, an uncanny
clank of chains resounded.

Help! The spectres dragged me away
and finally they bound me
fast at the foot of a mountain-face,
and who do you think found me?

Yes, it was that tassel again!
Still as filthy as ever,
now he looked like a vulture, sharp
of talon and black of feather,

and now like the Prussian eagle – his claws
were gripping me, unrelenting,
he was steadily eating my liver away,
I was groaning and lamenting.

Long I lamented – then the cock crew,
and my feverish dream subsided;
I lay in a sweat in that Minden bed,
the tassel hung harmless beside it.

I took the fast coach for Bückeburg,
and only out in the country
did I breathe again and begin to lose
the feeling of being hunted.

# XIX

O, Danton, du hast dich sehr geirrt
Und mußtest den Irrtum büßen!
Mitnehmen kann man das Vaterland
An den Sohlen, an den Füßen.

Das halbe Fürstentum Bückeburg
Blieb mir an den Stiefeln kleben;
So lehmigte Wege habe ich wohl
Noch nie gesehen im Leben.

Zu Bückeburg stieg ich ab in der Stadt,
Um dort zu betrachten die Stammburg,
Wo mein Großvater geboren ward;
Die Großmutter war aus Hamburg.

Ich kam nach Hannover um Mittagzeit,
Und ließ mir die Stiefel putzen.
Ich ging sogleich die Stadt zu besehn,
Ich reise gern mit Nutzen.

Mein Gott! da sieht es sauber aus!
Der Kot liegt nicht auf den Gassen.
Viel Prachtgebäude sah ich dort,
Sehr imponierende Massen.

Besonders gefiel mir ein großer Platz,
Umgeben von stattlichen Häusern;
Dort wohnt der König, dort steht sein Palast,
Er ist von schönem Äußern,

(Nämlich der Palast.) Vor dem Portal
Zu jeder Seite ein Schildhaus.
Rotröcke mit Flinten halten dort Wacht,
Sie sehen drohend und wild aus.

# XIX

O Danton, you were very wrong
and dearly you had to pay.
A man *can* take his country along,
when it's made of such sticky clay.

I had half the principality
of Bückeburg stuck to my boots;
I've never travelled in all my life
by half such muddy routes.

I got out in Bückeburg itself.
My grandpa was born in the town –
my grandmother came from Hamburg – it seemed
a reason for looking round.

My footwear was filthy. In Hanover
I had the mud scraped off it,
and out I went to inspect the town,
I like to travel with profit.

My goodness! That's a cleaner place,
the streets there don't need hosing.
It has some magnificent buildings too,
massive and very imposing.

What I specially liked was an open square
with stately homes and a palace,
the King of Hanover lives in it,
quite a reasonable one, on balance

(the palace, that is). Each side of the gate
it has a box with a sentry.
Redcoats with muskets stand on guard,
unsavoury-looking gentry.

Mein Cicerone sprach: »Hier wohnt
Der Ernst Augustus, ein alter,
Hochtoryscher Lord, ein Edelmann,
Sehr rüstig für sein Alter.

»Idyllisch sicher haust er hier,
Denn besser als alle Trabanten
Beschützet ihn der mangelnde Mut
Von unseren lieben Bekannten.

»Ich seh ihn zuweilen, er klagt alsdann,
Wie gar langweilig das Amt sei,
Das Königsamt, wozu er jetzt
Hier in Hannover verdammt sei.

»An großbritanisches Leben gewöhnt,
Sei es ihm hier zu enge,
Ihn plage der Spleen, er fürchte schier,
Daß er sich mal erhänge.

»Vorgestern fand ich ihn traurig gebückt
Am Kamin, in der Morgenstunde;
Er kochte höchstselbst ein Lavement
Für seine kranken Hunde.«


## XX

Von Harburg fuhr ich in einer Stund
Nach Hamburg. Es war schon Abend.
Die Sterne am Himmel grüßten mich,
Die Luft war lind und labend.

Und als ich zu meiner Frau Mutter kam,
Erschrak sie fast vor Freude;
Sie rief: »mein liebes Kind!« und schlug
Zusammen die Hände beide.

'This is where Ernst Augustus lives',
my guide took up his story,
'a nobleman, advanced in years,
but otherwise a Tory.

'He lives in idyllic safety here,
protected not by henchmen,
but by the lack of courage among
our friends, whose names I won't mention.

'Whenever I see him, he complains
how fearful borin' his job is,
being a king in Hanover
where this wretched German mob is.

'He's used to the British way of life,
he finds ours narrow beside it,
he suffers from spleen, and rather fears
he may hang himself now he's tried it.

'I recently found him at crack of dawn,
by his fireplace, stooping sadly,
his royal hands making a poultice for
his hounds, who'd caught something badly.'


# XX


From Harburg to Hamburg it took me about
an hour. The sun was setting.
The stars came out and greeted me,
the air was sweet and refreshing.

And when I came to my mother's house,
she was near overpowered with pleasure.
She cried 'My dearest boy!' and clapped
her dear old hands together.

117

»Mein liebes Kind, wohl dreizehn Jahr
Verflossen unterdessen!
Du wirst gewiß sehr hungrig sein –
Sag an, was willst du essen?

»Ich habe Fisch und Gänsefleisch
Und schöne Apfelsinen.«
So gib mir Fisch und Gänsefleisch
Und schöne Apfelsinen.

Und als ich aß mit großem Aptit,
Die Mutter ward glücklich und munter,
Sie frug wohl dies, sie frug wohl das,
Verfängliche Fragen mitunter.

»Mein liebes Kind! und wirst du auch
Recht sorgsam gepflegt in der Fremde?
Versteht deine Frau die Haushaltung,
Und flickt sie dir Strümpfe und Hemde?«

Der Fisch ist gut, lieb Mütterlein,
Doch muß man ihn schweigend verzehren;
Man kriegt so leicht eine Grät in den Hals,
Du darfst mich jetzt nicht stören.

Und als ich den braven Fisch verzehrt,
Die Gans ward aufgetragen.
Die Mutter frug wieder wohl dies, wohl das,
Mitunter verfängliche Fragen.

»Mein liebes Kind! in welchem Land
Läßt sich am besten leben?
Hier oder in Frankreich? und welchem Volk
Wirst du den Vorzug geben?«

Die deutsche Gans, lieb Mütterlein,
Ist gut, jedoch die Franzosen,
Sie stopfen die Gänse besser als wir,
Auch haben sie bessere Saucen. –

'My dearest boy! It's thirteen years
since last I had a look at you!
You must be very hungry, I'm sure –
just tell me what I can cook for you.

'I've got some fish and I've got some goose,
and some oranges to follow.'
'Then I'll have some fish and I'll have some goose,
and some oranges to follow.'

And as I sat there, tucking in,
my mother's cheerful talk would
keep turning to topics and touching on things
that I found distinctly awkward.

'Dear boy! Are you well looked after now?
I've heard that abroad it's shocking.
Does your wife know how to run a house,
can she darn a shirt and stocking?'

'This fish is excellent, mother dear,
but you mustn't disturb me with questions.
It's easy to swallow a bone if you talk,
and that's painful for people's digestions.'

And when I'd eaten the tasty fish,
the goose was next for serving.
My mother got on to her questions again,
some were a bit unnerving.

'My dearest boy! You've lived so long
in France, since your sudden removal.
Is it nicer there? Do the people and life
meet with your fuller approval?'

'Well, mother dear, the German goose
is good, but the French do stuffing
much better than we do, their sauces too
are famous, and not for nothing.'

Und als die Gans sich wieder empfahl,
Da machten ihre Aufwartung
Die Apfelsinen, sie schmeckten so süß,
Ganz über alle Erwartung.

Die Mutter aber fing wieder an
Zu fragen sehr vergnüglich,
Nach tausend Dingen, mitunter sogar
Nach Dingen, die sehr anzüglich.

»Mein liebes Kind! wie denkst du jetzt?
Treibst du noch immer aus Neigung
Die Politik? Zu welcher Partei
Gehörst du mit Überzeugung?«

Die Apfelsinen, lieb Mütterlein,
Sind gut, und mit wahrem Vergnügen
Verschlucke ich den süßen Saft,
Und ich lasse die Schalen liegen.


XXI


Die Stadt, zur Hälfte abgebrannt,
Wird aufgebaut allmählig;
Wie 'n Pudel, der halb geschoren ist,
Sieht Hamburg aus, trübselig.

Gar manche Gassen fehlen mir,
Die ich nur ungern vermisse –
Wo ist das Haus, wo ich geküßt
Der Liebe erste Küsse?

Wo ist die Druckerei, wo ich
Die Reisebilder druckte?
Wo ist der Austerkeller, wo ich
Die ersten Austern schluckte?

And when the goose had taken her leave,
for my further delectation
on came the oranges, juicy and sweet
beyond all expectation.

But my mother began her questions again –
you know how an old girl natters –
a thousand things she wanted to know,
among them some delicate matters.

'My dear boy! how do you see things now?
Do you still have your addiction
to politics? Which party now
commands your whole-hearted conviction?'

'These oranges, mother dear, are good,
so rich in tasty juices.
But I'm not inclined to swallow the peel,
the wrapping they come in is useless.'


## XXI

They're slowly rebuilding Hamburg – one half
was burnt in the fire disaster.
The town's now like a half-shorn dog,
looking sadly up at his master.

I'm sorry certain streets have gone,
there are places that one misses –
where is the house where my very first love
inspired my very first kisses?

Or the firm where my *Travel Sketches* saw print,
my first work, witty and boisterous?
Or that splendid oyster-cellar where
I swallowed my very first oysters?

Und der Dreckwall, wo ist der Dreckwall hin?
Ich kann ihn vergeblich suchen!
Wo ist der Pavillon, wo ich
Gegessen so manchen Kuchen?

Wo ist das Rathaus, worin der Senat
Und die Bürgerschaft gethronet?
Ein Raub der Flammen! Die Flamme hat
Das Heiligste nicht verschonet.

Die Leute seufzten noch vor Angst,
Und mit wehmütgem Gesichte
Erzählten sie mir vom großen Brand
Die schreckliche Geschichte:

»Es brannte an allen Ecken zugleich,
Man sah nur Rauch und Flammen!
Die Kirchentürme loderten auf
Und stürzten krachend zusammen.

»Die alte Börse ist verbrannt,
Wo unsere Väter gewandelt
Und mit einander Jahrhunderte lang
So redlich als möglich gehandelt.

»Die Bank, die silberne Seele der Stadt,
Und die Bücher, wo eingeschrieben
Jedweden Mannes Banko-Wert,
Gottlob! sie sind uns geblieben!

»Gottlob! man kollektierte für uns
Selbst bei den fernsten Nationen –
Ein gutes Geschäft – die Kollekte betrug
Wohl an die acht Millionen.

[Die Hilfsgelderkasse wurde geführt
Von wahren Christen und Frommen –
Erfahren hat nie die linke Hand,
Wieviel die rechte genommen.]

122

And Dirtwall, where is Dirtwall gone?
It isn't much use my looking.
Where's the Pavilion where they did
such marvellous pastry-cooking?

Where's the Town Hall where the Senate sat
and the Burgher Assembly debated?
It seems the most sacred things weren't spared,
that too was incinerated.

The people haven't recovered yet,
they were sighing and looking fearful.
They told me the terrible tale with faces
long and voices tearful:

'The fire was burning on every side,
there was smoke and flame all around;
the towers of churches blazed to the skies,
and came crashing down to the ground.

'The old Exchange was burnt right out,
where our ancestors through the ages
tried to lead honest business lives
without too much blotting their pages.

'The Bank, the city's silver soul,
and those books with the information
on what each man is worth, praise be!
were saved from the conflagration.

'Praise be! They collected on our behalf,
quite distant lands even sent some,
it added up to eight million in all –
for a whip-round, really quite handsome.

['The charity fund was run from the start
by Christians pious and true;
how much it was the right hand took,
the left hand never knew.]

»Aus allen Ländern floß das Geld
In unsre offnen Hände,
Auch Viktualien nahmen wir an,
Verschmähten keine Spende.

»Man schickte uns Kleider und Betten genug,
Auch Brot und Fleisch und Suppen!
Der König von Preußen wollte sogar
Uns schicken seine Truppen.

»Der materielle Schaden ward
Vergütet, das ließ sich schätzen –
Jedoch den Schrecken, unseren Schreck,
Den kann uns niemand ersetzen!«

Aufmunternd sprach ich: Ihr lieben Leut,
Ihr müßt nicht jammern und flennen,
Troja war eine bessere Stadt
Und mußte doch verbrennen.

Baut Eure Häuser wieder auf
Und trocknet Eure Pfützen,
Und schafft Euch beßre Gesetze an
Und beßre Feuerspritzen.

Gießt nicht zu viel Cayenne-Piment
In Eure Mokturtelsuppen,
Auch Eure Karpfen sind Euch nicht gesund,
Ihr kocht sie so fett mit den Schuppen.

Kalkuten schaden Euch nicht viel,
Doch hütet Euch vor der Tücke
Des Vogels, der sein Ei gelegt
In des Bürgermeisters Perücke. – –

Wer dieser fatale Vogel ist,
Ich brauch es Euch nicht zu sagen –
Denk ich an ihn, so dreht sich herum
Das Essen in meinem Magen.

'From every country the money flowed
into our open coffers.
They even sent us victuals too,
we didn't disdain any offers.

'People sent clothes and beds galore,
and bread and meat and soups too.
The King of Prussia even thought
he'd like to send us his troops too!

'The material damage was made good,
that was easily calculated –
but oh! the alarm, the fright we had,
that can never be compensated!'

I tried to cheer them: 'Dear people,' I said,
'It's no good weeping and wailing.
Troy was a better town, yet it burnt,
resistance was unavailing.

'Build your houses up again,
and dry up all the puddles,
get better hoses, and sort out
your fire-regulation muddles.

'Go easy on peppery mockturtle soup
and those dishes it's hard to stay thin on –
the carp you cook in that unhealthy way,
all swimming in fat, with the skin on.

'Turkey won't do you quite so much harm,
but beware! That other species
that's laid his egg in the Lord Mayor's wig
needs watching, he's malicious.

'Which vile bird that is, need I say?
I'm sure you catch my meaning.
I only have to think of him
and it sets my stomach heaving.'

125

# XXII

Noch mehr verändert als die Stadt
Sind mir die Menschen erschienen,
Sie gehn so betrübt und gebrochen herum,
Wie wandelnde Ruinen.

Die mageren sind noch dünner jetzt,
Noch fetter sind die feisten,
Die Kinder sind alt, die Alten sind
Kindisch geworden, die meisten.

Gar manche, die ich als Kälber verließ,
Fand ich als Ochsen wieder;
Gar manches kleine Gänschen ward
Zur Gans mit stolzem Gefieder.

Die alte Gudel fand ich geschminkt
Und geputzt wie eine Sirene;
Hat schwarze Locken sich angeschafft
Und blendend weiße Zähne.

Am besten hat sich konserviert
Mein Freund, der Papierverkäufer;
Sein Haar ward gelb und umwallt sein Haupt,
Sieht aus wie Johannes der Täufer.

Den ⁎⁎⁎⁎ den sah ich nur von fern,
Er huschte mir rasch vorüber;
Ich höre, sein Geist ist abgebrannt
Und war versichert bei Biber.

Auch meinen alten Zensor sah
Ich wieder. Im Nebel, gebücket,
Begegnet er mir auf dem Gänsemarkt,
Schien sehr darnieder gedrücket.

126

# XXII

I found the people of Hamburg changed
even more than the city,
like walking ruins they go about,
poor broken objects of pity.

The lean ones are much thinner now,
the stout ones have got still fatter,
the children have grown old, the adults
grown childish for that matter.

Some were now oxen I'd left as calves,
they'd clearly not had a lean time;
many a gosling had become
a proud-plumed goose in the meantime.

I found old Gudel all dolled up
and painted like a siren;
she'd acquired black locks and brilliant white teeth
you couldn't help admiring.

My friend the paper-seller was
the one who seemed to have kept best;
his hair has turned yellow, but still flows thick,
he looks like John the Baptist.

I only saw * * * go rushing by.
Poor man! If reports are reliable,
his mind was quite burned out, and his
insurers refused to be liable.

My dear old censor too I saw
again. In the mist, all stooping,
he met me in the Goosemarket,
his spirits were sadly drooping.

127

Wir schüttelten uns die Hände, es schwamm
Im Auge des Manns eine Träne.
Wie freute er sich, mich wieder zu sehn!
Es war eine rührende Szene. –


Nicht alle fand ich. Mancher hat
Das Zeitliche gesegnet.
Ach! meinem Gumpelino sogar
Bin ich nicht mehr begegnet.


Der Edle hatte ausgehaucht
Die große Seele soeben,
Und wird als verklärter Seraph jetzt
Am Throne Jehovahs schweben.


Vergebens suchte ich überall
Den krummen Adonis, der Tassen
Und Nachtgeschirr von Porzellan
Feil bot in Hamburgs Gassen.


Sarras, der treue Pudel, ist tot.
Ein großer Verlust! Ich wette,
Daß Campe lieber ein ganzes Schock
Schriftsteller verloren hätte. – –


Die Population des Hamburger Staats
Besteht, seit Menschengedenken,
Aus Juden und Christen; es pflegen auch
Die letztren nicht viel zu verschenken.


Die Christen sind alle ziemlich gut,
Auch essen sie gut zu Mittag,
Und ihre Wechsel bezahlen sie prompt,
Noch vor dem letzten Respittag.


Die Juden teilen sich wieder ein
In zwei verschiedne Parteien;
Die Alten gehn in die Synagog,
Und in den Tempel die Neuen.

We shook hands warmly, and a tear
welled under the old boy's eyelid.
He was so glad to see me again! He found
the occasion as touching as I did.

Not everyone was still about –
some are now 'dear departed';
I couldn't see Gumpelino again,
I felt quite broken-hearted.

The noble fellow's earthly span
was only quite recently over.
As a seraph transfigured he no doubt floats
by now round the throne of Jehovah.

Another old chap I tried to find
but couldn't come across again
was crooked Adonis, who strolled the streets
selling cups and nocturnal porcelain.

Sarras, the faithful hound, is no more.
A terrible loss! There's no doubting
that Campe would sooner have lost a score
of his authors than be without him.

The population of Hamburg State
has long been part Christian, part Jewish.
The Christians who ever give much away
are also decidedly fewish.

The Christians all are fairly good folk,
and at lunch-time they like good tucks-in.
They pay before creditors press too hard,
and stay solvent, as long as their luck's in.

The Jews can be subdivided again –
the distinction's really quite simple:
the old-style lot go to Synagogue,
and the new-fangled ones to the Temple.

Die Neuen essen Schweinefleisch,
Zeigen sich widersetzig,
Sind Demokraten; die Alten sind
Vielmehr aristokrätzig.

Ich liebe die Alten, ich liebe die Neun –
Doch schwör ich, beim ewigen Gotte,
Ich liebe gewisse Fischchen noch mehr,
Man heißt sie geräucherte Sprotte.


## XXIII

Als Republik war Hamburg nie
So groß wie Venedig und Florenz,
Doch Hamburg hat bessere Austern; man speist
Die besten im Keller von Lorenz.

Es war ein schöner Abend, als ich
Mich hinbegab mit Campen;
Wir wollten mit einander dort
In Rheinwein und Austern schlampampen.

Auch gute Gesellschaft fand ich dort,
Mit Freude sah ich wieder
Manch alten Genossen, zum Beispiel Chaufepié,
Auch manche neue Brüder.

Da war der Wille, dessen Gesicht
Ein Stammbuch, worin mit Hieben
Die akademischen Feinde sich
Recht leserlich eingeschrieben.

Da war der Fuchs, ein blinder Heid
Und persönlicher Feind des Jehovah,
Glaubt nur an Hegel und etwa noch
An die Venus des Canova.

New Jewry eats pork – when it comes to the Law,
they're great rebellion-backers;
they're democrats where the old-style Jews
are mostly aristocrackers.

I'm fond of them all, both new and old,
but I swear by the Holy Family
I'm even fonder of little smoked sprats –
that's a Hamburg speciality.


# XXIII


The Republic of Hamburg was never as great
as Venice, or as Florence;
but it has better oysters, the best can be had
at the excellent Keller 'Bei Lorenz'.

A beautiful evening it was when I
strolled down that way with Campe –
a publisher runs to oysters and hock
when he has his best author to pamper.

There was pleasant company gathered there.
I was glad to see, among others,
old comrades like Doctor Chaufepié,
and also several new brothers.

Wille was there, whose face is like
an autograph book, it's so dented
from student days, when his enemies' names
were very legibly entered.

There was Fuchs, a benighted infidel
and personal foe of Jehovah;
he only believes in Hegel, and p'raps
the Venus of Canova.

Mein Campe war Amphitryo
Und lächelte vor Wonne;
Sein Auge strahlte Seligkeit,
Wie eine verklärte Madonne.

Ich aß und trank, mit gutem Aptit,
Und dachte in meinem Gemüte:
»Der Campe ist wirklich ein großer Mann,
Ist aller Verleger Blüte.

»Ein andrer Verleger hätte mich
Vielleicht verhungern lassen,
Der aber gibt mir zu trinken sogar;
Werde ihn niemals verlassen.

»Ich danke dem Schöpfer in der Höh,
Der diesen Saft der Reben
Erschuf, und zum Verleger mir
Den Julius Campe gegeben!

»Ich danke dem Schöpfer in der Höh,
Der, durch sein großes Werde,
Die Austern erschaffen in der See
Und den Rheinwein auf der Erde!

»Der auch Zitronen wachsen ließ,
Die Austern zu betauen –
Nun laß mich, Vater, diese Nacht
Das Essen gut verdauen!«

Der Rheinwein stimmt mich immer weich
Und löst jedwedes Zerwürfnis
In meiner Brust, entzündet darin
Der Menschenliebe Bedürfnis.

Es treibt mich aus dem Zimmer hinaus,
Ich muß in den Straßen schlendern;
Die Seele sucht eine Seele und späht
Nach zärtlich weißen Gewändern.

My Campe sat with a genial grin
and revelled in doing the honours;
his visage shone with bliss, just like
those saintly transfigured madonnas.

I ate and drank most heartily,
and thought to myself, indistinctly:
'Old Campe is really a very great man,
among publishers he's princely.

'Another one might have abandoned me
in a garret, starving and pining.
I shall always stick to Campe. With him,
there's wining as well as dining.

'Thanks be to the Almighty on high
for making the grape and its juices,
and for giving me Julius Campe to print
the works my pen produces!

'Thanks be to the Almighty on high
whose fiat set in motion
the Rhineland hock-trade, and brought forth
the oysters in the ocean!

'Who also made the lemons grow
to add to the oysters' attraction –
Father, preserve my stomach this night
from any violent reaction!'

Hock always gets me going, a mood
of benevolence and urbanity
comes over me, I feel the need
to express my love of humanity.

It drives me out of doors, I have
to go out in the streets a-strolling,
my soul seeks another soul – will there be
any long white garments patrolling?

In solchen Momenten zerfließe ich fast
Vor Wehmut und vor Sehnen;
Die Katzen scheinen mir alle grau,
Die Weiber alle Helenen. – – –

Und als ich auf die Drehbahn kam,
Da sah ich im Mondenschimmer
Ein hehres Weib, ein wunderbar
Hochbusiges Frauenzimmer.

Ihr Antlitz war rund und kerngesund,
Die Augen wie blaue Turkoasen,
Die Wangen wie Rosen, wie Kirschen der Mund,
Auch etwas rötlich die Nase.

Ihr Haupt bedeckte eine Mütz
Von weißem gesteiftem Linnen,
Gefältelt wie eine Mauerkron,
Mit Türmchen und zackigen Zinnen.

Sie trug eine weiße Tunika,
Bis an die Waden reichend.
Und welche Waden! Das Fußgestell
Zwei dorischen Säulen gleichend.

Die weltlichste Natürlichkeit
Konnt man in den Zügen lesen;
Doch das übermenschliche Hinterteil
Verriet ein höheres Wesen.

Sie trat zu mir heran und sprach:
»Willkommen an der Elbe,
Nach dreizehnjährger Abwesenheit –
Ich sehe, du bist noch derselbe!

»Du suchst die schönen Seelen vielleicht,
Die dir so oft begegent
Und mit dir geschwärmt die Nacht hindurch,
In dieser schönen Gegend.

At moments like these I almost melt
with melancholy and yearning;
all cats are grey in the dark, all women
are Helens, I'm not too discerning.

And when I came to the Drehbahn, I saw
there in the moonlight, majestic,
a splendid figure of womanhood,
wondrously large-breasted.

Her face was round and bespoke rude health,
her eyes they were turquoise blue,
her cheeks were like roses, like cherries her lips,
her nose was reddish too.

Upon her head she wore a cap
with elaborate decorations –
starched white linen, folded and tucked
into towers and crenellations.

She wore a tunic of white, which reached
to her calves. What calves they were, too!
A Doric column's the only apt
comparison I can refer to.

A naturalness that was quite of this world
was writ in her face for the seeing;
but the superhuman hinderparts
betrayed a higher being.

She accosted me, and thus she spoke:
'Welcome to Hamburg once more
after thirteen years away. I observe
you have the same tastes as before.

'You're looking perhaps for the Beautiful Souls
who would meet you by Elbe's water
and spend the gay night hours with you
down here in this pleasant quarter.

[»Du suchst vergebens! Du findest nicht mehr
Die lange Male, die dicke
Posaunenengel-Hannchen, du findest auch nicht
Die Braunschweiger Mummen-Friedrike.

»Du suchst vergebens! Du findest nicht mehr
Den Schimmel, die falsche Marianne,
Pique-Aß-Luise, die rote Sophie,
Auch nicht die keusche Susanne.

»Du findest die Strohpuppen-Jette nicht mehr,
Nicht mehr die große Malwine,
Auch nicht die Kuddelmuddel-Marie,
Auch nicht die Dragoner-Kathrine.]

»Du findest die holden Blumen nicht mehr,
Die das junge Herz vergöttert;
Hier blühten sie – jetzt sind sie verwelkt,
Und der Sturm hat sie entblättert.

»Verwelkt, entblättert, zertreten sogar
Von rohen Schicksalsfüßen –
Mein Freund, das ist auf Erden das Los
Von allem Schönen und Süßen!«

»Das Leben verschlang sie, das Ungetüm,
Die unersättliche Hyder;
Du findest nicht die alte Zeit
Und die Zeitgenössinnen wieder!

[»Seitdem du uns verlassen hast,
Hat manches sich hier verwandelt,
Es wuchs ein junges Geschlecht heran,
Das anders fühlt und handelt.

»Die Reste der Vergangenheit
Verwittern und verschwinden,
Du wirst jetzt auf der Schwiegerstraß
Ein neues Deutschland finden.«

['But Long Moll's gone, and Chubby-cheeked Nan's
gone too, in vain you'll seek her,
nor will you find the Brunswick lass
known as Fancy-dress Frederica.

'You'll seek in vain, for gone as well
are Ace-of-Spades Lou, Miss Whitey,
Red-headed Sophie, Chastity Sue
and Marianna the Flighty.

'And Straw-haired Hetty's no longer about,
and nor is Big Malvina.
And Madcap Mary's no more seen
than Battleaxe Katrina.]

'You'll find no more those flowers pure
your young heart was always adoring;
they blossomed here, they are faded now,
their petals blown down by the stormwind.

'Faded, plucked, trod down indeed
by Fate with its brutal feet –
my friend, that is the lot on earth
of everything lovely and sweet.

'They've been swallowed up by that monster Life,
the hundred-headed hydra;
you won't get back those good old times,
or the girls who enjoyed them beside you.

['After you left us, things began
to change beyond recognising;
the way young people feel and act
today I find deeply surprising.

'What's left of the Germany we knew
has been left to wither and weather,
if you go down Schwieger Street, you'll find
a different world altogether.'

137

Wer bist du – rief ich – daß du kennst
Die Namen jener Damen,
Die an des Jünglings Bildung einst
Den tätigsten Anteil nahmen?

Ja, ich gesteh, es hängt mein Herz
Ein bißchen an dem alten
Deutschland noch immer, ich denke noch gern
An die schönen verlornen Gestalten.]

Wer bist du? – rief ich – du schaust mich an
Wie 'n Traum aus alten Zeiten –
Wo wohnst du, großes Frauenbild?
Und darf ich dich begleiten?

Da lächelte das Weib und sprach:
»Du irrst dich, ich bin eine feine,
Anständge, moralische Person;
Du irrst dich, ich bin nicht so Eine.

»Ich bin nicht so eine kleine Mamsell,
So eine welsche Lorettin –
Denn wisse: ich bin Hammonia,
Hamburgs beschützende Göttin!

»Du stutzest und erschreckst sogar,
Du sonst so mutiger Sänger!
Willst du mich noch begleiten jetzt?
Wohlan, so zögre nicht länger.«

Ich aber lachte laut und rief:
Ich folge auf der Stelle –
Schreit du voran, ich folge dir,
Und ging es in die Hölle!

'Who are you,' I cried, 'that you know the names
of that Hamburg generation
who in bygone nights took an active hand
in my early education?

'I have to admit, I do still have
a soft spot for the old ways,
for Germany as it was, and for all
those lovely girls from the old days.]

'But you, who are you? You look at me
like a dream from days beyond telling –
where do you live, great lady, and may
I escort you back to your dwelling?'

The woman smiled, and thus she spoke:
'You're mistaken, Sir, I'm a good
respectable, moral person, and not
one of *that* sisterhood.

'I'm not a girlie, as you suppose,
not one of your French-style totties.
Know this: I am Hammonia,
Hamburg's Guardian Goddess.

'I see you falter, I see you are shocked,
you who were once a bold singer.
D'you still wish to see me home? If so,
then kindly do not linger.'

But I, I laughed aloud and cried:
'I will follow without delay –
lead on forthwith, I will follow you
though Hell should bar the way!'

139

# XXIV

Wie ich die enge Sahltrepp hinauf
Gekommen, ich kann es nicht sagen;
Es haben unsichtbare Geister mich
Vielleicht hinaufgetragen.

Hier, in Hammonias Kämmerlein,
Verflossen mir schnell die Stunden.
Die Göttin gestand die Sympathie,
Die sie immer für mich empfunden.

»Siehst du« – sprach sie – »in früherer Zeit
War mir am meisten teuer
Der Sänger, der den Messias besang
Auf seiner frommen Leier.

»Dort auf der Kommode steht noch jetzt
Die Büste von meinem Klopstock,
Jedoch seit Jahren dient sie mir
Nur noch als Haubenkopfstock.

»Du bist mein Liebling jetzt, es hängt
Dein Bildnis zu Häupten des Bettes;
Und, siehst du, ein frischer Lorbeer umkränzt
Den Rahmen des holden Porträtes.

»Nur daß du meine Söhne so oft
Genergelt, ich muß es gestehen,
Hat mich zuweilen tief verletzt;
Das darf nicht mehr geschehen.

»Es hat die Zeit dich hoffentlich
Von solcher Unart geheilet,
Und dir eine größere Toleranz
Sogar für Narren erteilet.

# XXIV

How I got up those narrow stairs
I find quite mystifying;
perhaps invisible spirits bore
me up them, as if flying.

Up in Hammonia's little room
I hardly noticed the time pass.
The goddess confessed to me how strong
her liking for me and my rhyme was.

'The poet,' she said, 'who in earlier times
I most warmly used to admire
was the bard whose pious measures told
the story of the Messiah.

'Look over there at the sideboard – the bust
of dear Klopstock still stands upon it,
although for years it's only been used
to keep the shape in my bonnet.

'Now you are my favourite, your portrait hangs
at the head of my bed – with bay-leaves
you see the picture-frame is crowned,
I dust and adjust them daily.

'I must admit, though, the fact that you
kept needling my sons with such frequency
has often wounded me deeply – it went
beyond the bounds of decency.

'I hope you will have learned by now
not to behave so badly,
you ought to be more tolerant
and suffer fools more gladly.

»Doch sprich, wie kam der Gedanke dir,
Zu reisen nach dem Norden
In solcher Jahrzeit? Das Wetter ist
Schon winterlich geworden!«

O, meine Göttin! – erwiderte ich –
Es schlafen tief im Grunde
Des Menschenherzens Gedanken, die oft
Erwachen zur unrechten Stunde.

Es ging mir äußerlich ziemlich gut,
Doch innerlich war ich beklommen,
Und die Beklemmnis täglich wuchs –
Ich hatte das Heimweh bekommen.

Die sonst so leichte französische Luft,
Sie fing mich an zu drücken;
Ich mußte Atem schöpfen hier
In Deutschland, um nicht zu ersticken.

Ich sehnte mich nach Torfgeruch,
Nach deutschem Tabaksdampfe;
Es bebte mein Fuß vor Ungeduld,
Daß er deutschen Boden stampfe.

Ich seufzte des Nachts, und sehnte mich,
Daß ich sie wiedersähe,
Die alte Frau, die am Dammtor wohnt;
Das Lottchen wohnt in der Nähe.

Auch jenem edlen alten Herrn,
Der immer mich ausgescholten
Und immer großmütig beschützt, auch ihm
Hat mancher Seufzer gegolten.

Ich wollte wieder aus seinem Mund
Vernehmen den »dummen Jungen!«
Das hat mir immer wie Musik
Im Herzen nachgeklungen.

'But tell me, there's one thing I'm puzzled about,
there must be a special reason
why you came back home in weather like this?
Winter is scarcely the season.'

'The human heart, o Goddess' – said I –
'is deep and enigmatic.
Its impulses come at the awkwardest times,
it's really quite erratic.

'Outwardly everything seemed all right,
but within there was something amiss with me,
it was homesickness, a bad attack,
I thought of my homeland wistfully.

'Like lead the French air weighed on me
which once was so stimulating;
I had to breathe German air again,
for fear of suffocating.

'I yearned for the fug from German pipes,
for the reek of burning peat;
I trembled with eagerness to have
German soil under my feet.

'At night I sighed and longed to see
my mother, I sorely missed her,
the old girl who lives by the Dam Gate, near
dear Lottie, that's my sister.

'And also that noble old gentleman
whose generous protection
and regular scoldings I once enjoyed.
Some sighs went in his direction.

'I wanted to hear him say "Young fool!" –
That was once his favourite phrase;
like music it's always rung in my heart
as an echo of far-off days.

Ich sehnte mich nach dem blauen Rauch,
Der aufsteigt aus deutschen Schornsteinen,
Nach niedersächsischen Nachtigalln,
Nach stillen Buchenhainen.

Ich sehnte mich nach den Plätzen sogar,
Nach jenen Leidensstationen,
Wo ich geschleppt das Jugendkreuz
Und meine Dornenkronen.

Ich wollte weinen, wo ich einst
Geweint die bittersten Tränen –
Ich glaube, Vaterlandsliebe nennt
Man dieses törigte Sehnen.

Ich spreche nicht gern davon; es ist
Nur eine Krankheit im Grunde.
Verschämten Gemütes, verberge ich stets
Dem Publiko meine Wunde.

Fatal ist mir das Lumpenpack,
Das, um die Herzen zu rühren,
Den Patriotismus trägt zur Schau
Mit allen seinen Geschwüren.

Schamlose schäbige Bettler sinds,
Almosen wollen sie haben –
Ein'n Pfennig Popularität
Für Menzel und seine Schwaben!

O meine Göttin, du hast mich heut
In weicher Stimmung gefunden;
Bin etwas krank, doch pfleg ich mich,
Und ich werde bald gesunden.

Ja, ich bin krank, und du könntest mir
Die Seele sehr erfrischen
Durch eine gute Tasse Tee;
Du mußt ihn mit Rum vermischen.

144

'I yearned to see the blue smoke again
that rises from German chimneys,
for Lower Saxony's nightingales,
and those quiet groves of beech-trees.

'I even yearned for the places that once
were the stations of my passion,
where I dragged my cross and wore my thorns –
my youthful suffering's ration.

'I wanted to weep where once I felt
the bitterest tear-drops burning –
it's a kind of patriotism, I
suppose, this foolish yearning.

'I don't like to mention it; at root
it's a disease, this feeling,
a wound that I'm ashamed of, and not
a thing for public revealing.

'There's nothing I hate like that villainous pack
who, to stir up easy emotions,
flaunt their patriotism about
and lay bare their ulcerous notions.

'Shameless beggars is what they are,
shabbily seeking charity.
All Menzel and the Swabians want
is a penn'orth of popularity.

'O Goddess, today I was in the mood
for rather giving way to it;
I have the disease, but I'm treating myself
and I shall soon put paid to it.

'Yes, I am sick – a cup of tea
I would take as a friendly favour;
that's the refreshment my spirit needs.
Just add some rum for flavour.'

# XXV

Die Göttin hat mir Tee gekocht
Und Rum hineingegossen;
Sie selber aber hat den Rum
Ganz ohne Tee genossen.

An meine Schulter lehnte sie
Ihr Haupt (die Mauerkrone,
Die Mütze, ward etwas zerknittert davon)
Und sie sprach mit sanftem Tone:

»Ich dachte manchmal mit Schrecken dran,
Daß du in dem sittenlosen
Paris so ganz ohne Aufsicht lebst,
Bei jenen frivolen Franzosen.

»Du schlenderst dort herum und hast
Nicht mal an deiner Seite
Einen treuen deutschen Verleger, der dich
Als Mentor warne und leite.

»Und die Verführung ist dort so groß,
Dort gibt es so viele Sylphiden,
Die ungesund, und gar zu leicht
Verliert man den Seelenfrieden.

»Geh nicht zurück und bleib bei uns;
Hier herrschen noch Zucht und Sitte,
Und manches stille Vergnügen blüht
Auch hier, in unserer Mitte.

»Bleib bei uns in Deutschland, es wird dir hier
Jetzt besser als ehmals munden;
Wir schreiten fort, du hast gewiß
Den Fortschritt selbst gefunden.

# XXV

The Goddess made me tea with rum,
I sat and watched her see to it;
as for herself, she drank the rum
without adding any tea to it.

Then when we'd had our refreshment, she leaned
her head upon my shoulder
(her fancy cap got crumpled a bit)
and replied to what I had told her:

'I often thought of you living there
among that frivolous nation,
all alone with no friend to preserve
you from all that immoral temptation.

'You stroll about the Paris streets
and don't even have beside you
a faithful German publisher, as
a mentor to warn and guide you.

'Seduction there is hot and strong,
all those sylphs on the look-out for gallants,
their health isn't all it ought to be,
and a young man can quite lose his balance.

'Don't go back to France, stay with us instead;
here there's self-control and propriety,
and many quieter pleasures too,
to add a bit of variety.

'Stay here – the Germany of today
you'll find much more to your liking;
we're very progressive, I'm sure you've found
the signs of progress striking.

»Auch die Zensur ist nicht mehr streng,
Hoffmann wird älter und milder
Und streicht nicht mehr mit Jugendzorn
Dir deine Reisebilder.

»Du selbst bist älter und milder jetzt,
Wirst dich in manches schicken,
Und wirst sogar die Vergangenheit
In besserem Lichte erblicken.

»Ja, daß es uns früher so schrecklich ging,
In Deutschland, ist Übertreibung;
Man konnte entrinnen der Knechtschaft, wie einst
In Rom, durch Selbstentleibung.

»Gedankenfreiheit genoß das Volk,
Sie war für die großen Massen,
Beschränkung traf nur die gringe Zahl
Derjengen, die drucken lassen.

»Gesetzlose Willkür herrschte nie,
Dem schlimmsten Demagogen
Ward niemals ohne Urteilspruch
Die Staatskokarde entzogen.

»So übel war es in Deutschland nie,
Trotz aller Zeitbedrängnis –
Glaub mir, verhungert ist nie ein Mensch
In einem deutschen Gefängnis.

»Es blühte in der Vergangenheit
So manche schöne Erscheinung
Des Glaubens und der Gemütlichkeit;
Jetzt herrscht nur Zweifel, Verneinung.

»Die praktische äußere Freiheit wird einst
Das Ideal vertilgen,
Das wir im Busen getragen – es war
So rein wie der Traum der Liljen!

'The censorship is no longer strict,
Hoffmann's got older, he stretches
a point, he's not the angry young man
who hacked your *Travel Sketches*.

'You're older and mellower yourself,
you too will be more easy-going,
you'll see even the past in a rosier light
than on your previous showing.

'That things were ever so terrible here
is simply an overstatement;
you could always opt for suicide
if you couldn't put up with enslavement.

'The people enjoyed full freedom of thought,
at least among the masses,
restrictions only affected the
small group of the writing classes.

'The vilest demagogues, who went
among the people and stirred it –
they were never exiled out of hand,
there was always a legal verdict.

'To talk of oppression and tyranny
is a wild exaggeration –
no prisoner in a German gaol
was left to die of starvation.

'Consider the German past: so many
lovely examples it offers
of simple faith and harmony.
Now we're plagued with doubters and scoffers.

'This practical outward freedom, you'll see,
will kill the ideal we cherish,
our dream of Germany lily-pure –
we shall have to watch it perish.

»Auch unsre schöne Poesie
Erlischt, sie ist schon ein wenig
Erloschen; mit andern Königen stirbt
Auch Freiligraths Mohrenkönig.

»Der Enkel wird essen und trinken genug,
Doch nicht in beschaulicher Stille;
Es poltert heran ein Spektakelstück,
Zu Ende geht die Idylle.

»O, könntest du schweigen, ich würde dir
Das Buch des Schicksals entsiegeln,
Ich ließe dir spätere Zeiten sehn
In meinen Zauberspiegeln.

»Was ich den sterblichen Menschen nie
Gezeigt, ich möcht es dir zeigen:
Die Zukunft deines Vaterlands –
Doch ach! du kannst nicht schweigen!«

Mein Gott, o Göttin! – rief ich entzückt –
Das wäre mein größtes Vergnügen,
Laß mich das künftige Deutschland sehn –
Ich bin ein Mann und verschwiegen.

Ich will dir schwören jeden Eid,
Den du nur magst begehren,
Mein Schweigen zu verbürgen dir –
Sag an, wie soll ich schwören?

Doch jene erwiderte: »Schwöre mir
In Vater Abrahams Weise,
Wie er Eliesern schwören ließ,
Als dieser sich gab auf die Reise.

»Heb auf das Gewand und lege die Hand
Hier unten an meine Hüften,
Und schwöre mir Verschwiegenheit
In Reden und in Schriften!«

'Our poetry too is burning low,
if not yet quite extinguished;
Freiligrath's Moorish King will die out,
with kings that are more distinguished.

'Our children will eat and drink their fill,
but it won't be our old-world idyll;
a Big Spectacular's on the way
which will cut it off short in the middle.

'If you could keep a secret, I
would unseal Destiny's book for you,
in my magic mirrors the future's revealed;
I could arrange a look for you.

'I have never shown it to mortal eye,
but to you I should like to show it:
the future of your Fatherland –
but alas! you'd let everyone know it.'

'Good God, o Goddess,' I cried in delight,
'it would be a supreme pleasure,
let me see Germany as it will be –
I will guard your secret like treasure.

'I will swear before you whatever oath
you care to ask of me, whereby
to guarantee full secrecy –
pray tell me, what shall I swear by?'

But she then answered: 'Swear the oath
Father Abraham exacted
when he sent his man Eliezer to get
a wife for Isaac contracted.

'Lift up my garment and lay your hand
here on my thigh beneath it,
and swear that in writing and in speech
you will keep what I show you secret.'

Ein feierlicher Moment! Ich war
Wie angeweht vom Hauche
Der Vorzeit, als ich schwur den Eid,
Nach uraltem Erzväterbrauche.

Ich hob das Gewand der Göttin auf
Und legte an ihre Hüften
Die Hand, gelobend Verschwiegenheit
In Reden und in Schriften.


## XXVI

Die Wangen der Göttin glühten so rot
(ich glaube, in die Krone
Stieg ihr der Rum), und sie sprach zu mir
In sehr wehmütigem Tone:

»Ich werde alt. Geboren bin ich
Am Tage von Hamburgs Begründung.
Die Mutter war Schellfischkönigin
Hier an der Elbe Mündung.

»Mein Vater war ein großer Monarch,
Carolus Magnus geheißen,
Er war noch mächtger und klüger sogar
Als Friedrich der Große von Preußen.

»Der Stuhl ist zu Aachen, auf welchem er
Am Tage der Krönung ruhte;
Den Stuhl, worauf er saß in der Nacht,
Den erbte die Mutter, die gute.

»Die Mutter hinterließ ihn mir,
Ein Möbel von scheinlosem Äußern,
Doch böte mir Rothschild all sein Geld,
Ich würde ihn nicht veräußern.

A solemn moment! I felt the breath
of ancient times on my visage
as I stood before her and swore the oath
after the patriarch's usage.

I lifted the Goddess's garment and laid
my hand on her thigh beneath it,
and swore that in writing and in speech
I would keep what she showed me secret.


# XXVI

The Goddess's cheeks were red and flushed –
the rum, I think, was doing it –
and thus she spoke, in saddened tones,
as if she was already ruing it:

'I grow old, for I was born the day
they founded Hamburg, the daughter
of an estuary haddock-queen
down by the Elbe's broad water.

'My father was great Charlemagne,
the lord of a mighty kingdom.
He had even more power than Frederick the Great
of Prussia, and much more wisdom.

'The throne he sat on the day he was crowned
is still in Aachen; the other,
the one he sometimes sat on at night,
was left to my dear late mother.

'My mother left it in turn to me:
as antiques go, there are finer,
but I wouldn't swap it for Rothschild's bank
or for all the tea in China.

153

»Siehst du, dort in dem Winkel steht
Ein alter Sessel, zerrissen
Das Leder der Lehne, von Mottenfraß
Zernagt das Polsterkissen.

»Doch gehe hin und hebe auf
Das Kissen von dem Sessel,
Du schaust eine runde Öffnung dann,
Darunter einen Kessel –

»Das ist ein Zauberkessel, worin
Die magischen Kräfte brauen,
Und steckst du in die Ründung den Kopf,
So wirst du die Zukunft schauen –

»Die Zukunft Deutschlands erblickst du hier,
Gleich wogenden Phantasmen,
Doch schaudre nicht, wenn aus dem Wust
Aufsteigen die Miasmen!«

Sie sprachs und lachte sonderbar,
Ich aber ließ mich nicht schrecken,
Neugierig eilte ich den Kopf
In die furchtbare Ründung zu stecken.

Was ich gesehn, verrate ich nicht,
Ich habe zu schweigen versprochen,
Erlaubt ist mir zu sagen kaum,
O Gott! was ich gerochen! – – –

Ich denke mit Widerwillen noch
An jene schnöden, verfluchten
Vorspielgerüche, das schien ein Gemisch
Von altem Kohl und Juchten.

Entsetzlich waren die Düfte, o Gott!
Die sich nachher erhuben;
Es war, als fegte man den Mist
Aus sechsunddreißig Gruben. – – –

'It's over there in the corner, look,
just an old chair; the leather
is worn and torn on the arms, the seat
is moth-eaten altogether.

'But if you go across and lift
· the cushion from the settle,
you'll see a circular opening,
and beneath it a pot made of metal.

'That is a magic pot, wherein
the occult forces are brewing;
if you put your head down the hole, it will be
the future you are viewing –

'The future of Germany you will see
down there like a shifting phantasma,
but do not shudder if the filth
sends up a foul miasma!'

Thus she spake, and laughed a strange laugh;
but I was not to be daunted.
Curious, I hastened to peer through the hole,
to see what terrors would haunt it.

What I saw, I will not betray,
for I promised never to tell it.
But seeing was only half the tale –
Ye gods! if you could smell it! . . .

It still revolts me when I recall
the smells I smelt to begin with –
the stink of untanned hides, and of old
bad cabbage it was mixed in with.

But the scents that followed this prelude, God!
were anything but respites;
it smelt as if they were sweeping the dung
from six-and-thirty cesspits.

Ich weiß wohl, was Saint-Just gesagt
Weiland im Wohlfahrtsausschuß:
Man heile die große Krankheit nicht
Mit Rosenöl und Moschus –

Doch dieser deutsche Zukunftsduft
Mocht alles überragen,
Was meine Nase je geahnt –
Ich konnt es nicht länger ertragen – – –

Mir schwanden die Sinne, und als ich aufschlug
Die Augen, saß ich an der Seite
Der Göttin noch immer, es lehnte mein Haupt
An ihre Brust, die breite.

Es blitzte ihr Blick, es glühte ihr Mund,
Es zuckten die Nüstern der Nase,
Bacchantisch umschlang sie den Dichter und sang
Mit schauerlich wilder Ekstase:

»Bleib bei mir in Hamburg, ich liebe dich,
Wir wollen trinken und essen
Den Wein und die Austern der Gegenwart,
Und die dunkle Zukunft vergessen.

»Den Deckel darauf! damit uns nicht
Der Mißduft die Freude vertrübet –
Ich liebe dich, wie je ein Weib
Einen deutschen Poeten geliebet!

»Ich küsse dich, und ich fühle, wie mich
Dein Genius begeistert;
Es hat ein wunderbarer Rausch
Sich meiner Seele bemeistert.

»Mir ist, als ob ich auf der Straß
Die Nachtwächter singen hörte –
Es sind Hymenäen, Hochzeitmusik,
Mein süßer Lustgefährte!

I know that curing a great disease
is harder than one supposes –
as Saint-Just once said, you don't get far
with musk and oil of roses.

But the way the German future smelt
was ghastly, hideous – stronger
than ever my nose had bargained for –
soon I could stand it no longer . . .

I lost my senses, and when once more
I opened my eyes, the Goddess
was there beside me, my head reposed
upon her buxom bodice.

Her eyes were flashing, her lips aglow,
her breath came fast and frantic;
she sang a wild ecstatic song
as she clasped me in embrace bacchantic:

'Stay with me in Hamburg, I love you, let's
attend to the eating and drinking of
oysters and wine in the present, the dark
German future doesn't bear thinking of.

'Put back the lid! It would dampen our joys
if that smell crept out from below it.
I love you as hotly as woman e'er loved
a handsome German poet.

'The moment I kiss you, I'm carried away
by poetic inspiration,
I feel my soul is in the grip
of a wondrous intoxication.

'I seem to hear out there in the street
the nightwatchmen singing for us –
sweet partner in pleasure, they're marriage songs,
an epithalamial chorus!

157

»Jetzt kommen die reitenden Diener auch,
Mit üppig lodernden Fackeln,
Sie tanzen ehrbar den Fackeltanz,
Sie springen und hüpfen und wackeln.

»Es kommt der hoch- und wohlweise Senat,
Es kommen die Oberalten;
Der Bürgermeister räuspert sich
Und will eine Rede halten.

»In glänzender Uniform erscheint
Das Korps der Diplomaten;
Sie gratulieren mit Vorbehalt
Im Namen der Nachbarstaaten.

»Es kommt die geistliche Deputation,
Rabbiner und Pastöre –
Doch ach! da kommt der Hoffmann auch
Mit seiner Zensorschere!

»Die Schere klirrt in seiner Hand,
Es rückt der wilde Geselle
Dir auf den Leib – Er schneidet ins Fleisch –
Es war die beste Stelle.«

## XXVII

Was sich in jener Wundernacht
Des Weitern zugetragen,
Erzähl ich Euch ein andermal,
In warmen Sommertagen.

Das alte Geschlecht der Heuchelei
Verschwindet Gott sei Dank heut,
Es sinkt allmählig ins Grab, es stirbt
An seiner Lügenkrankheit.

'And now I see mounted servants appear,
with torches suggestively flickering,
they dance the torch-dance to honour us,
jumping and prancing and wiggling.

'The City Elders and Senate are come,
that reverend institution;
the Burgomaster clears his throat
to pronounce an allocution.

'The corps of diplomats appears,
they're resplendent for the formalities
and (with some reservations) wish us well
in the name of their principalities.

'The rabbis and pastors are here in force
to represent things religious –
Oh dear! here's Censor Hoffmann too,
and he's brought his official scissors!

'The scissors are clicking in his hand –
he's wild, he's foaming, he's hissing –
he rushes up to you – there's a snip –
alack! now your best piece is missing.'


# XXVII


What happened subsequently on
that wondrous nocturnal occasion
I'll save for warmer summer days
and separate narration.

The Grundy generation now
thank Heaven is slowly dying,
it's ripe for the grave, brought low by its own
hypocrisy and lying.

Es wächst heran ein neues Geschlecht,
Ganz ohne Schminke und Sünden,
Mit freien Gedanken, mit freier Lust –
Dem werde ich Alles verkünden.

Schon knospet die Jugend, welche versteht
Des Dichters Stolz und Güte,
Und sich an seinem Herzen wärmt,
An seinem Sonnengemüte.

Mein Herz ist liebend wie das Licht,
Und rein und keusch wie das Feuer;
Die edelsten Grazien haben gestimmt
Die Saiten meiner Leier.

Es ist dieselbe Leier, die einst
Mein Vater ließ ertönen,
Der selige Herr Aristophanes,
Der Liebling der Kamönen.

Es ist die Leier, worauf er einst
Den Paisteteros besungen,
Der um die Basileia gefreit,
Mit ihr sich emporgeschwungen.

Im letzten Kapitel hab ich versucht
Ein bißchen nachzuahmen
Den Schluß der »Vögel«, die sind gewiß
Das beste von Vaters Dramen.

Die »Frösche« sind auch vortrefflich. Man gibt
In deutscher Übersetzung
Sie jetzt auf der Bühne von Berlin,
Zu königlicher Ergetzung.

Der König liebt das Stück. Das zeugt
Von gutem antiken Geschmacke;
Den Alten amüsierte weit mehr
Modernes Froschgequacke.

A new generation is rising that has
no hang-ups or pretences;
it thinks what it likes, enjoys what it likes –
I will help it keep its senses.

The youth now budding will understand
the benevolence of a proud poet,
his heart has the warmth of a radiant sun,
he is eager to bestow it.

My heart is loving as the light,
and pure and chaste as fire;
the noblest of the graces have tuned
the strings that span my lyre.

It is the lyre my father struck
that now his offspring uses –
the great Greek Aristophanes,
the darling of the Muses.

It is the lyre with which he sang
of how Pisthetairos courted
Basileia, and both at last
together were exalted.

In chapter twenty-six, I tried
a modest imitation
of the final scene of father's *Birds* –
that's his very finest creation.

*The Frogs* is also a splendid piece.
They're playing a German version
at present on the Berlin stage,
for the King's own royal diversion.

The King enjoys the play. That shows
some taste – for an ancient poet.
But when modern frogs begin to croak,
he doesn't want to know it.

Der König liebt das Stück. Jedoch
Wär noch der Autor am Leben,
Ich riete ihm nicht sich in Person
Nach Preußen zu begeben.

Dem wirklichen Aristophanes,
Dem ginge es schlecht, dem Armen;
Wir würden ihn bald begleitet sehn
Mit Chören von Gendarmen.

Der Pöbel bekäm die Erlaubnis bald
Zu schimpfen statt zu wedeln;
Die Polizei erhielte Befehl
Zu fahnden auf den Edeln.

O König! Ich meine es gut mit dir
Und will einen Rat dir geben:
Die toten Dichter, verehre sie nur,
Doch schone die da leben.

Beleidge lebendige Dichter nicht,
Sie haben Flammen und Waffen,
Die furchtbarer sind als Jovis Blitz,
Den ja der Poet erschaffen.

Beleidge die Götter, die alten und neun,
Des ganzen Olymps Gelichter,
Und den höchsten Jehovah obendrein –
Beleidge nur nicht den Dichter!

Die Götter bestrafen freilich sehr hart
Des Menschen Missetaten,
Das Höllenfeuer ist ziemlich heiß,
Dort muß man schmoren und braten –

Doch Heilige gibt es, die aus der Glut
Losbeten den Sünder; durch Spenden
An Kirchen und Seelenmessen wird
Erworben ein hohes Verwenden.

The King enjoys the play. But if
the author were still living,
the welcome he'd get in Prussia would not
be the same his play's been given.

The real Aristophanes, poor chap,
would no sooner have crossed our border
than we'd see him getting a short, sharp shock
from the forces of law and order.

The mob, instead of applauding, would soon
abuse him, at higher behest;
and in no time at all there'd be warrants out
for the noble fellow's arrest.

O King! I have your welfare at heart,
this is good advice I'm giving:
by all means honour the poets of yore –
but watch your step with the living.

Don't rub live poets up the wrong way;
they have weapons that make Jove's lightning
(a poet invented that) look tame.
If you cross them, your prospects are frightening.

Offend the gods, the old and the new,
Zeus and all his pack up
high on Olympus, Jehovah as well –
but don't get the poet's back up.

The gods have punishments harsh enough
for human evil-doing,
the fires of Hell are pretty hot,
you sit there braising and stewing –

Still, there are saints to pray you free
from the cooking-fires of the Devil;
donations to churches and masses for souls
win friends at the Highest level.

Und am Ende der Tage kommt Christus herab
Und bricht die Pforten der Hölle;
Und hält er auch ein strenges Gericht,
Entschlüpfen wird mancher Geselle.

Doch gibt es Höllen, aus deren Haft
Unmöglich jede Befreiung;
Hier hilft kein Beten, ohnmächtig ist hier
Des Welterlösers Verzeihung.

Kennst du die Hölle des Dante nicht,
Die schrecklichen Terzetten?
Wen da der Dichter hineingesperrt,
Den kann kein Gott mehr retten –

Kein Gott, kein Heiland erlöst ihn je
Aus diesen singenden Flammen!
Nimm dich in Acht, daß wir dich nicht
Zu solcher Hölle verdammen.

And when time's ended, Christ will come
to snatch away Hell's portion;
it's true his judgment will be stern,
still, some will get off with a caution.

But there are hells whose inmates are doomed
to stay imprisoned forever;
prayer won't avail, and powerless is
the Saviour's loving endeavour.

Have you not heard of Dante's Hell,
the terrible *terza rima*?
Whoever has once been shut in there
can hope for no redeemer.

The poet's flames have got him for good,
they scorch and scourge and scorn him.
Take care: we might roast you in just such a hell
as an everlasting warning.

# PARALIPOMENA

## *Abschied von Paris*

Ade, Paris, du teure Stadt,
Wir müssen heute scheiden,
Ich lasse dich im Überfluß
Von Wonne und von Freuden.

Das deutsche Herz in meiner Brust
Ist plötzlich krank geworden,
Der einzige Arzt, der es heilen kann,
Der wohnt daheim im Norden.

Er wird es heilen in kurzer Frist,
Man rühmt seine großen Kuren;
Doch ich gestehe, mich schaudert schon
Vor seinen derben Mixturen.

Ade, du heitres Franzosenvolk,
Ihr meine lustigen Brüder,
Gar närrische Sehnsucht treibt mich fort,
Doch komm ich in Kurzem wieder.

Denkt Euch, mit Schmerzen sehne ich mich
Nach Torfgeruch, nach den lieben
Heidschnucken der Lüneburger Heid,
Nach Sauerkraut und Rüben.

Ich sehne mich nach Tabaksqualm,
Hofräten und Nachtwächtern,
Nach Plattdeutsch, Schwarzbrot, Grobheit sogar,
Nach blonden Predigerstöchtern.

Auch nach der Mutter sehne ich mich,
Ich will es offen gestehen,
Seit dreizehn Jahren hab ich nicht
Die alte Frau gesehen.

# PARALIPOMENA

## *Departure from Paris*

Paris, farewell, beloved town,
today I have to leave you
in all your rich abundance of
pleasure and *joie de vivre*.

The German heart within my breast
a-suddenly is ailing;
only one doctor in the north
can cure it without failing.

His cure it will be prompt and sure,
he has that reputation;
his bitter mixtures, though, I grant,
fill me with trepidation.

Farewell, you jolly Frenchmen all,
it is a foolish yearning
that drives me from you, brothers in fun,
but I shan't be long returning.

Just think, I yearn to smell the peat,
see heathland sheep, taste sauer-
kraut, turnips and black rye bread, and hear
the watchman call the hour.

I miss the pipesmoke, dialect,
pompous officials, rudeness,
and German daughters of the manse
in all their blond-haired cuteness.

I long to see my mother too –
you'll think this no dishonour –
through all these thirteen exile years
I've not set eyes upon her.

Ade, mein Weib, mein schönes Weib,
Du kannst meine Qual nicht fassen,
Ich drücke dich so fest an mein Herz,
Und muß dich doch verlassen.

Die lechzende Qual, sie treibt mich fort
Von meinem süßesten Glücke –
Muß wieder atmen deutsche Luft,
Damit ich nicht ersticke.

Die Qual, die Angst, der Ungestüm,
Das steigert sich bis zum Krampfe.
Es zittert mein Fuß vor Ungeduld,
Daß er deutschen Boden stampfe.

Vor Ende des Jahres bin ich zurück
Aus Deutschland, und ich denke
Auch ganz genesen, ich kaufe dir dann
Die schönsten Neujahrsgeschenke.

## Zu XXVI

Die Äser, die schon vermodert längst
Und nur noch historisch gestunken,
Sie dünsteten aus ihr letztes Gift,
Halb Tote, halb Halunken.

Und gar das heilige Gespenst,
Die auferstandene Leiche,
Die ausgesogen das Lebensblut
Von manchem Volk und Reiche,

Sie wollte noch einmal verpesten die Welt
Mit ihrem Verwesungshauche!
Entsetzliche Würmer krochen hervor
Aus ihrem faulen Bauche –

Und jeder Wurm ein neuer Vampir,
Der wieder tödlich gerochen,
Als man ihm durch den schnöden Leib
Den heilsamen Pfahl gestochen.

Farewell my wife, my lovely wife,
you cannot know my torture;
I press you to me tenderly,
but I can't delay departure.

A torturing thirst drives me away,
although you love me so sweetly –
I have to breathe German air again
or I'll suffocate completely.

Within me the torments of eagerness
stronger and stronger surge,
and to set foot on German soil again
is an irresistible urge.

By the end of the year, I'll be cured and back
to enjoy my convalescence,
and then I'll buy you – very first thing –
the nicest New Year presents.


## XXVI: ? *after stanza 11*

The carrion of history, villains long past
and ancient corpses, still noisome
though long since rotted, were giving off
the final whiff of their poison.

And they were outdone by that holy ghost,
the resurrected vampire
which has sucked the very life-blood of
so many a people and empire.

It was out to infect the world again
with its breath that sets all things decaying.
Its rotten belly gaped open wide,
the horrible worms displaying;

and every worm a vampire in turn
which added its stinking bit to
the general stench, when its hideous form
was caught and safely slit through.

Es roch nach Blut, Tabak und Schnaps
Und nach gehenkten Schuften –
Wer übelriechend im Leben war,
Wie mußt er im Tode duften!

Es roch nach Pudeln und Dachsen und auch
Nach Mopsen, die zärtlich gelecket
Den Speichel der Macht und fromm und treu
Für Thron und Altar verrecket.

Das war ein giftiger Moderdunst,
Entstiegen dem Schinderpfuhle –
Drin lag die ganze Hundezunft,
Die ganze historische Schule.


\*    \*


»Es ist ein König in Thule, der hat
'nen Becher, nichts geht ihm darüber,
Und wenn er aus dem Becher trinkt,
Dann gehen die Augen ihm über.

»Dann steigen in ihm Gedanken auf,
Die kaum sich ließen ahnden,
Dann ist er kapabel und dekretiert,
Auf dich, mein Kind, zu fahnden.

»Geh nicht nach Norden, und hüte dich
Vor jenem König in Thule,
Hüt dich vor Gendarmen und Polizei,
Vor der ganzen historischen Schule.

A stink of blood, tobacco and schnaps
and of criminals hung for atrocities –
in life they were evil-smelling enough,
in death they were stinking monstrosities.

A stink of hounds and bitches, a stink
of lap-dogs whose pious loyalty
would lick the spittle of Power, and die
for Altar and for Royalty.

A poisonous stench of rotting it was
that that knacker's heap exuded;
there the beastly school of Historical Law
its earthly span concluded.


XXVI: *? after stanza 17*


'A King there is in Thule, he has
a goblet, 'tis what he holds dearest,
and when from the goblet he has drunk,
his vision is not of the clearest.

'Then thoughts arise in his fuddled mind
which others would find abhorrent,
and soon, my child, you may find your name
inscribed on a Prussian warrant.

'So don't go near that northern King,
keep safely out of his way,
look out for the gendarmes and police
and the lawyers he has in his pay . . . '

# NOTES

Page 31 St. 3: *belly . . . hands.* Good fighting talk at first sight –
but can organs of the same body have conflicting interests? Not
if we take at face value the metaphor of a single harmonious
'body politic'. The plebs in Shakespeare's *Coriolanus (I, i)* do
when the Senator Menenius placates them with a fable of how the
limbs once rebelled against the belly: the belly claimed it only
received 'the general food at first' and sent out the goodness
equally to all the body, retaining 'but the bran'; and 'the Senators
of Rome are that good belly.' Has Heine, who knew his
Shakespeare, scored an own goal and invalidated his own
rhetoric? Only if we too swallow the metaphor uncritically. If we
recognise the allusion, 'belly' and 'hands' remind us how the
plebs were duped, and raise the question of how internally
harmonious the body politic really is.

Page 33 St. 4: *the giant.* One of Hercules' labours was to kill the
giant Antaeus, whose strength was renewed if he touched his
mother Earth. Schiller's poem 'The Three Illusions' ('Die Worte
des Wahns') made that an image of idealism defeating the real
world:

> 'You must strangle him clear of the ground, for then
> He cannot grow strong from earth's touch again.'

Heine, strikingly, makes Antaeus the hero. The reversal is in
tune with his earthier values.

Page 35 St. 4: August Heinrich *Hoffmann von Fallersleben.*
Contemporary political poet.

Page 35 St. 5: *Zollverein.* The Customs Union was a Prussian
initiative, taken in 1828 to create some economic unity between
German states. Prussia's declining power-competitor, Austria,
saw it (rightly) as a move to strengthen Prussian political
influence.

Page 35 St. 7: *Empire of you-know-when.* The so-called Holy
Roman Empire of the German Nation, the only previous form of
(loose and largely ineffective) German unity, was dissolved by
Napoleon in 1806.

Page 35 St. 7: *to the censor.* Strict censorship laws were among the repressive measures taken by the German princes in the Karlsbad Decrees of 1819.

Page 37 St. 1: *Karl Mayer.* Heine liked to mock the rural-provincial poets of the Swabian School. Reading 'Mayer' as a form of the Latin 'major', this minor poet's name can (just about) mean 'Carolus Magnus', or Charlemagne.

Page 37 St. 5: Theodor *Körner.* The best-known of the patriotic poets of the Wars of Liberation (1813–15) against Napoleon. His 'Song of the Black Chasseurs' contains the stanza:

> 'Still mourn we with our black and vengeful coats
> Our lost courageous dead.
> But if folk ask you what the red denotes,
> 'Tis French blood that we shed.'

Page 37 St. 7: *the corporal's stick.* Symbol of the severe discipline in the Prussian army under Old Fritz, i.e. Frederick the Great.

Page 39 St. 4: *Lady Jane . . .* Heroine of a play of that name, sub-titled 'Romantic Portrait from the Fourteenth Century', by August von Kotzebue.

Page 41 St. 2: *that bird.* The Prussian eagle, of course. One of several points where censorship or self-censorship removed the explicit identification.

Page 43 St. 4: *Men Obscure.* The *Letters of Obscure Men* (*Epistolae obscurorum virorum,* 1515-17) was an anonymous satire on church abuses, in the form of an apparent – stupid – defence of the Church. The Reformation polemicist *Ulrich von Hutten* was one of the authors.

Page 43 St. 5: Jakob van *Hogstraeten,* organiser of the Cologne Inquisition c. 1510, was one of Hutten's targets, especially for burning Jewish books. Wolfgang *Menzel,* a writer originally well-disposed towards Heine and other liberals, was involved in the campaign against them which led to their being identified and banned as a group ('Young Germany') by a decree of the Confederation of German States in 1835. Heine published an attack on Menzel entitled 'The Informer' in 1837.

Page 43 St. 7: *theological hatred.* Toned down on the advice of friends from the original 'anti-semitic hatred'. Given the historical background Heine recalls, the point stays the same in substance.

Page 45 St. 2: *half-constructed.* Building began in the thirteenth century, was interrupted during the Reformation, and only completed through the favourable conjunction of medievalism (the original building-plans were published by Sulpiz Boisserée in the 1820s) and the religiosity of the Prussian King Friedrich Wilhelm IV, whose rule now extended to the Rhineland.

Page 45 St. 5: *Jews, of all people*: probably a rueful reference to Heine himself. He was actually for a time Vice-President of an Association for the Completion of Cologne Cathedral in Paris – one more symptom of Heine's intriguingly divided mind.

Page 47 St. 2: *bones of the Three Wise Men.* Relics brought back from Milan in 1164 by the then Bishop of Cologne. The container can still be inspected behind the High Altar of Cologne Cathedral.

Page 47 St. 5: *Tailor-King.* Nickname of the sixteenth-century Anabaptist Jan van Leyden, who was executed with two of his followers and exposed as Heine describes.

Page 47 St. 7: *Holy Alliance.* The Holy Alliance of Heine's time was originally a declaration of Christian principles by the Tsar, the Austrian Emperor and the King of Prussia in 1815, but was soon a catchword for the reactionary policies conducted or inspired by Metternich.

Page 47 St. 8: *promise a constitution.* It was a standing, and true, accusation of liberals against the German princes that they had inveigled their subjects into fighting against Napoleon in the Wars of Liberation by just such enticements.

Page 49 St. 7: *swallowed some stones.* In 1841, stone probably meant for Cologne Cathedral was sunk by one petty state (Hesse-Darmstadt) to close the new harbour built at Bieberich by another petty state (Hesse-Nassau). A nice instance of German Lilliputian politics.

Page 49 St. 7: *Becker's verse.* The famous poem beginning 'They shall not take it from us, our free and German Rhine' (1840) was provoked, it must be admitted, by another build-up of the recurrent nineteenth-century French ambition to make the Rhine once more the Franco-German border.

Page 51 St. 8: *Alfred de Musset.* The French Romantic writer produced a poem in reply to Becker's, 'Le Rhin allemand'.

Page 53 St. 4: *philosophers now.* The French interest in German literature and thought goes back to Madame de Staël's *De l'Allemagne* of 1813, but was stimulated anew by the French versions of Heine's own *Romantic School* (1835) and *History of Religion and Philosophy in Germany* (1836) – both of them, despite the serious titles, overflowing with wit and liveliness as well as deeply perceptive.

Page 53 St. 4: *beer-house games.* For Heine, the excessive abstraction of German thought was complemented by the complacent materialism of German middle-class philistines. In his poem 'No need to worry' ('Zur Beruhigung') he makes a chorus of them draw a reassuring contrast with the Roman republicans, who were 'tyrant-eaters':

> 'We are no Romans, we like a smoke –
> Tastes do differ from folk to folk,
> Every people is great at something,
> In Swabia they cook you the finest dumpling.'

Page 53 St. 7: *without ever seeming to make it.* Musset's many involvements, including George Sand and the Princesse de Belgiojoso, make it uncertain just how the list would read.

Page 55 St. 1: *George Harris.* Despite the name, a German journalist who became Paganini's secretary.

Page 61 St. 2: *abstract notions.* Much of Heine's work is an effort to understand the relation – and overcome the split – between the worlds of thought and action. Were Germany's spiritual and philosophical revolutions (Luther's, Kant's) alternatives to real revolution or preparation for it? The dream that now follows is an optimistic answer.

Page 69 St. 1: *Scrawny Brotherhood.* By the post-Napoleonic settlement of 1815, Prussia acquired Rhineland territory stretching from the Dutch and Westphalian borders in the north to the borders of Lorraine and Bavaria in the south.

Page 69 St. 6: *resurrected since.* Napoleon's remains were transferred from St Helena and placed in the Invalides on 15 December 1840.

Page 73 St. 5: *decorated with laurels.* The wolves, in Caput XII, doubt Heine's integrity. This is his own attack on the conformists who stayed at home and prospered in a repressive society.

Page 75 St. 3: *Göttingen days.* Heine studied at the University of Göttingen in two phases (separated by a spell of rustication for duelling) in the early 1820s. His account of a walking tour

176

through the Harz mountains (*Die Harzreise*, 1826) opens with a description of 'the town of Göttingen, famous for its sausages and University'. (Both are still excellent.)

Page 75 St. 6: *from . . . deeds of daring.* Part of the anti-heroic tradition that goes back to Falstaff (*Henry IV*, Part 1, V, i, the sceptical speech about 'honour'), includes Shaw's 'chocolate soldier' Bluntschli in *Arms and the Man*, and is represented in German by Brecht's *Mother Courage*, especially scene ii: 'If the general could make a good plan, what'd he need brave soldiers for? Ordinary 'uns would do. [. . .] In a good country, you don't have to have virtues, everyone can be completely ordinary, just middling-clever, and for all I care cowards.'

Page 77 St. 2: *Arminius . . . Hermann.* The search for German legendary figures to counter French cultural hegemony in the eighteenth century, and to inspire patriots in the fight against French military power in 1813–15, brought to light this ancient vanquisher of the Romans. Klopstock (see Caput XXIV) published a drama *Hermann's Battle* in 1769, and Heinrich von Kleist wrote another of the same title in 1808 which, with its obvious reference to the Napoleonic present, could not be published till 1821. The patriotic poetry of the Wars of Liberation also made liberal use of Hermann's name and example.

Page 77 Sts 5 ff: *Hengstenberg*, et al. We hardly need explanations of the personal names in Caput XI in order to enjoy it (if, indeed, explanatory notes can ever *make* satire enjoyable where it isn't already). We can infer very roughly what Heine's victims stand for in their society, while the notion of a 'Roman reversal' of German history groups them into a playful unity with its own zest and coherence. This then makes up a single large comment on the ideals and illusions of the nationalists, in the light of the ironic question in St. 3 on this page: 'Would German liberty be what it is?'

Ernst Wilhelm *Hengstenberg:* Protestant Professor of Theology in Berlin. Johann August Wilhelm *Neander:* Professor of Evangelical Church History in Berlin. Charlotte *Birch-Pfeiffer:* actress and author of light plays. Friedrich von *Raumer:* jurist and historian, of harmless revolutionary pretensions. Ferdinand *Freiligrath*: one of the would-be political poets. *Father Jahn*: Friedrich Ludwig Jahn, founder of the German gymnastics movement, which aimed at regeneration, physical and moral, of the German people during the French occupation and was thus a kind of covert resistance organisation. Hans Ferdinand *Massmann:* another patriotic gymnast and specialist in Germanic studies. Friedrich Wilhelm *Schelling:* philosopher, deeply suspect in Heine's eyes as the first to move from abstruse metaphysics to a justification of the existing social order; it is therefore doubly incongruous to think of him committing suicide Roman style, as the philosopher and playwright Seneca did in the repressive reign of Nero. Peter von *Cornelius:* painter, of the Nazarene school which inclined to religious allegory.

Page 79 St. 4: *Cacatum non est pictum.* 'Shitting isn't painting', a proverbial saying of at least sixteenth-century origin for achievement that falls short of ambition (not just in painting).

Page 81 St. 1: *monument.* Begun 1838, completed 1875.

Page 81 St. 7: '. . . *fellow wolves* . . .' Even while defending himself against his suspicious allies, Heine manages also to parody the vacuity of political speechifying, at least for the first two stanzas. There is again a Peter Sellers parallel, in the record of a 'Party Political Speech' consisting of sweet nothings.

Page 83 St. 8: Gustav *Kolb* was editor-in-chief of the *Augsburger Allgemeine Zeitung* in which Heine published a good deal of his journalism, especially the articles which later made up the volumes *Conditions in France* of 1832 (reports on the aftermath of the July Revolution) and *Lutezia* of 1854.

Page 85 St. 1: *near Paderborn.* Heine's attack on institutionalised religion in Caput I is taken further by appropriating Jesus for the radical, anti-Establishment cause. If, as a thumbnail sketch in the history of ideas, you take Christian ethics as the source of Enlightenment humanitarianism, and the Enlightenment as the source of Heine's liberal-socialist principles, his claim has some plausibility. Behind the seemingly blasphemous familiarity, Heine's irony this time is ultimately benign.

Page 87 St. 5: *ancient song.* No exactly corresponding folksong has been identified, though there are similar motifs in a fairy-story from the collection of the Brothers Grimm, number 115: 'The clear sun brings it to light'.

Page 89 St. 4: *loneliest of princesses.* See number 89 of the Grimms' collection, 'The goose-girl'.

Page 91 St. 1: *Emperor-in-Hiding.* The legend of a past hero who will return in his country's hour of need (cf. Sir Henry

Newbolt's poem 'Drake's Drum') was adaptable to various political purposes, and Heine was not the first, or last, to invoke Barbarossa (it was the codename of Hitler's invasion of Russia in 1941). His sense of being in dubious company is one reason why he feels unsure about the Emperor as his ally.

Page 101 St. 4: *Moses Mendelssohn.* Jewish philosopher, friend of Lessing, and one of the leading figures of the German Enlightenment; grandfather of the composer Felix.

Page 101 St. 7: Anna Louise *Karschin,* Karoline Luise von *Klencke,* Helmine von *Chezy.* Writers.

Page 109 St. 2: *Lawcourts.* Heine had studied law, and thought at one time of writing a book on medieval theories of the state. The point here is the difference between a knowledge of what the Middle Ages were really like, and the Romantic idealisation which ignored their darker side.

Page 113 St. 4: *mountain-face.* The captured poet falls into the role of Prometheus, who stole fire from the gods and was chained by Zeus to a rock in the Caucasus; there an eagle daily ate at his liver, which was restored at night.

Page 115 St. 1: Georges *Danton,* the French revolutionary leader, refused to flee France when his friends warned him against Robespierre's plotting: 'Partir? Est-ce qu'on emporte sa patrie à la semelle de son soulier?' He was tried and guillotined.

Page 117 St. 1: *Ernst Augustus.* Duke of Cumberland and leader of the Tory lords before succeeding to the throne of Hanover. He aimed to restore absolutist, not to say feudal government, and in 1837 abolished a constitution granted by his predecessor. This gave rise to the protest of the 'Göttingen Seven' – a group of professors including the Brothers Grimm – which the King answered by dismissing them. Heine's choice of an individual ruler to focus attention on was a good one.

Page 121 St. 5: *fire disaster.* On 5–8 May 1842, a third of the Inner City was destroyed, fifty-one people killed, and 20,000 made homeless.

Page 121 St. 7: *'Travel Sketches'.* Heine's *Reisebilder* of the 1820s – *Journey through the Harz, The North Sea, Ideas: Le Grand's Book, From Munich to Genoa* and *The Baths of Lucca* – took the old travelogue form, added wit and sentiment in the manner of Laurence Sterne's *Sentimental Journey*, and took licence to digress at any moment on any subject. A lot of political and social points were made, easy to spot for the quick reader but able to slip past a dozy censor. The link with *Deutschland is* obvious, and Heine called his poem 'versified travel-sketches'.

Page 123 St. 8: *pious and true.* Did Heine leave out this – technically very successful – stanza because it was too offensive in his own publisher's locality? or because the charge wasn't true? I include it so as to pose the problem. (There *is* an art-for-art's-sake – or malice for malice's sake – side to satirists.)

Page 125 St. 2: *send us his troops too!* Not only thought, but did. They were meant to help keep order and control the fire. Pressure was also put on the Free City to join the Customs Union. The bird in Sts 7 and 8 is the Prussian eagle again.

Page 127 St. 4: *Gudel* and the other figures in Caput XXII and Caput XXIII are too minor (and self-explanatory) to be worth annotating. The fun lies, as in the 'Roman' Caput XI, in the way Heine plays with motifs, here the usually serious ones of time and mutability.

Page 129 st 5: Julius *Campe,* of the firm Hoffmann & Campe, published almost all Heine's works in his lifetime, and the first collected editions after his death. Without a base in a Free City like Hamburg, Heine could have achieved little in Germany. His relations with Campe were compounded of common interest, solidarity, affection and mutual mistrust – i.e. it was a typical author-publisher relationship. Publishers find authors difficult and demanding, and fear they will take their best works elsewhere; authors are touchy about how their works are edited, printed and promoted (Campe's need to deal with the censor complicated things even more in this case) and are liable to suspect that the publisher is making a lot more money than they themselves are. When not worried by all of this (which however he was for most of the time) Heine felt warmly towards Campe. *Deutschland* captures some of these fleeting moments. Alcohol (see Caput XXIII) helped. Hoffmann & Campe, incidentally, are the publishers of one of the new standard editions of Heine now in progress.

Page 131 St. 6: *legibly entered.* I.e. as duelling scars. The German student practice was (and in some places again is) to fence with eyes protected but cheeks exposed, in the hope of picking up lifelong evidence of gallantry.

Page 135 St. 2: *Drehbahn.* A street with a reputation comparable to that of the Reeperbahn today.

Page 137 Sts 4 and 5: *blown down by the stormwind . . . everything lovely and sweet.* Two allusions to famous scenes – the ending of Lessing's *Emilia Galotti* and Thekla's epitaph on her lover Max in Schiller's *Wallenstein* – create a humour of incongruity.

Page 137 St. 8: *Schwieger Street.* As for Drehbahn (see note to page 135 St. 2). Hamburg was well provided.

Page 141 St. 3: *the Messiah.* A poem of that name, twenty cantos in hexameters published between 1748 and 1773, was the main life's work of Friedrich Gottlieb *Klopstock* (St. 4).

Page 141 St. 6: *needling my sons.* This reaction to criticism, and the plea for an idyllic view of Germany in Caput XXV, make a serious social and political point about attitudes in Heine's day, and well beyond. Literature with the critical function that has long been normal in France and Britain has always had to struggle for attention, let alone acceptance, in Germany.

Page 143 St. 7: *noble old gentleman.* Heine's uncle, the rich Hamburg banker Salomon Heine, with at least one of whose daughters Heine is traditionally supposed to have been in love. The tone here is mild, but there were other moods, in one of which Heine summed up his bitter experience of his uncle's house and its inhabitants in the poem 'Castle Contumely' *(Affrontenburg).* At the most basic level, Heine knew Uncle Salomon could have transformed his always precarious literary existence with a sum the rich man would not have noticed. Heine might then well have written less.

Page 145 St. 6: *Menzel and the Swabians.* See notes to page 37 St. 1 and page 43 St. 5. The attacks on the writers of 'Young Germany' claimed impeccable patriotic motives.

Page 149 St. 4: *full freedom of thought.* Another literary allusion, to the scene in Schiller's *Don Carlos* where Marquis Posa appeals to Philip II of Spain to grant 'freedom of thought' throughout his dominions.

Page 149 St. 6: *die of starvation.* If true, this ignores the fact that there were those who died of torture, like Pastor Weidig, a friend of the dramatist Georg Büchner in the state of Hesse-Darmstadt, where they distributed a political pamphlet. What contemporary readers would know is the basis for Heine's ironic effect.

Page 151 St. 1: *Moorish King.* On Freiligrath, see Caput XI. This particular poem stuck in Heine's gullet especially, and figures (too largely) in *Atta Troll.*

Page 153 St. 6: *sat on at night.* The idea of connecting Charlemagne's night-stool with prophecies of the German future just may have come from one of the patriotic poems of 1813–15, Max von Schenkendorf's 'The Chair of Charlemagne', which contains the lines:

> 'In his spirit never dreaming
> What dark threads the future wove . . .'

The idea of being sworn to secrecy about the future's exact course was a neat tactic of Heine's for not committing himself to a prophecy events might falsify. Simply, given the accumulated nastiness of Germany's 'six-and-thirty cesspits', the necessary historical change was bound to stir up a stink.

Page 155 St. 8: *six-and-thirty cesspits.* Perhaps another whiff of myth here – another of the labours of Hercules was to clean out the Augean stables.

Page 157 St. 1: Antoine de *Saint-Just.* French revolutionary politician and close associate of Robespierre. But the aphorism – 'Voulez-vous qu'on fasse des révolutions à l'eau de rose?' – was apparently coined by Chamfort.

Page 167 Sts 1 ff: *Paris, farewell . . .* The main interest of this discarded introduction is how closely it matches the 1836 poem 'Der Tannhauser', in both style – a much less spring-heeled movement, with far fewer of the crucial unstressed syllables, than in the final text; and themes – living in (unsatisfying) pleasure, travelling to find bitterness, parting from a loved woman. It was writable, and very possibly written, before Heine left Paris, and before he had the new 'Antaean' experience of return from exile to generate a new and more vigorous mode.

Page 169 Sts 5 ff: *The carrion of history . . .* It looks rather as if Heine began to elaborate on the vision Hammonia had granted him, but then realised that this meant breaking the oath he had taken in the fiction not to tell a soul what he saw. There were also stylistic reasons for abandoning the sequence – see Introduction, page 17.

Page 169 St. 6: *that holy ghost.* Perhaps the restored *ancien régime*, with its claim to 'divine right'; perhaps the Church in its habitual alliance with absolutist (or indeed any temporal) power. Cf. also St. 6 of this sequence.

Page 171 St. 3: *school of Historical Law.* Historians of Roman Law, most prominent among them Friedrich Karl von Savigny (at this time Prussian Minister of Justice), treated time-honoured laws as immutable and reform as inadmissible. 'A school which brands as rebellion the cry of the serf against the lash as soon as that lash can be shown to be an ancient, historical, inherited lash,' as Karl Marx said in his *Critique of Hegel's Philosophy of Right*, 1844.

# FURTHER READING

Anyone who feels an addiction to Heine coming on can find the whole of his poetry in translation in Hal Draper, *The Complete Poems of Heinrich Heine. A Modern English Version*, Oxford University Press 1982. Draper's gallant commitment to rendering the entire oeuvre, rather than working by mood and fancy as the opportunist does, inevitably means the quality is uneven. But there are plenty of good versions, and the overall achievement is monumental. For a first sampling of Heine's shorter poems, including political pieces in the spirit of *Deutschland*, try the selection in David Cram and T. J. Reed, *Heinrich Heine*, Everyman Poetry 1997. The entertainment of Heine's prose should not be missed, since it is some of the lightest and most readable in the German language. See the recent version, *Heinrich Heine. Selected Prose*, translated and edited by Ritchie Robertson, Penguin Classics 1993.

An excellent account in English of Heine's life is the American scholar Jeffrey Sammons's *Heinrich Heine. A Modern Biography*, Princeton and Manchester 1979. There has been a lot of good critical writing in English on Heine, whose dislike of England has never been reciprocated. He has always been popular in the Anglo-Saxon world at large, not just with German specialists, and often for the qualities that have made him seem suspect to many Germans: wit, irony, critical intelligence, a healthy disrespect for authority. Eminent Victorians had their reservations, but still recognised his significance. Matthew Arnold, unsurprisingly, found Heine wanting in 'nobleness of soul and character', yet could not fail to see that 'in the European literature of that quarter of a century which follows the death of Goethe' in 1832, Heine was 'incomparably the most important figure.' Arnold's essay of 1863 and the earlier one by George Eliot, 'German Wit: Heinrich Heine' of 1856, combine penetration and perspective and still make excellent starting points.

Of my dedicatee S. S. Prawer's critical work on Heine, the most directly relevant to the poem *Deutschland* is *Heine the Tragic Satirist*, Cambridge 1961. But there is also much fascinating detail and insight into satirical technique in two later studies: *Heine's*

*Jewish Comedy*, Oxford 1983, and *Frankenstein's Island. England and the English in the writings of Heinrich Heine*, Cambridge 1986. Barker Fairley's *Heinrich Heine. An Interpretation*, Oxford 1954, follows the thread of theatrical and performance images that runs through all Heine's writing. William Rose, *Heinrich Heine. Two Studies of his Thought and Feeling*, Oxford 1956, looks into Heine's social attitudes and Jewish heritage. Ritchie Robertson, *Heine*, London 1988, in the series 'Jewish Thinkers', is a concise account, especially of Heine's intellectual world. The political and social themes of *Deutschland* are seen in the whole complex of Heine's oeuvre in Nigel Reeves, *Heinrich Heine. Poetry and Politics*, Oxford 1974, reprinted by Libris, London 1994. They are related to continuities in German history through the succession of case-histories offered in Hans Kohn's *The Mind of Germany*, New York and London 1965, and in Gordon A. Craig's similarly structured book *The Politics of the Unpolitical: German Writers and the Problem of Power 1770–1871*, Oxford 1995, where the long-standing German refusal to recognise Heine is concisely recounted. The fuller historical background is provided, again with particular attention to the German intellectual world, in James Sheehan's *German History 1770–1866*, Oxford 1989. The medievalism of the German Romantics is described in W. H. Robson Scott's *The Literary Background of the Gothic Revival in Germany*, Oxford 1965. An intriguing creative response to the emblematic figure of Heine as Jew, writer, and exile is Tony Harrison's *The Gaze of the Gorgon*, Newcastle 1992, a long poem that originated as a BBC television film. Heine is here made the speaker of a bitter monologue that surveys twentieth-century, especially German, history.

185

## ANGEL BOOKS

A Select List

Angel Books publishes classic foreign literature in new translations that aim to recreate the impact of the original texts in versions that live in English. Critical introductions and any necessary annotation are provided. Angel Books' programme focuses on authors and works not currently or adequately available in English.

For a complete list of titles please write to Angel Books, 3 Kelross Road, London N5 2QS

# Poetry

GENNADY AYGI
Selected Poems 1954–94
*Bilingual edition; with translations, introduction and notes by*
*Peter France*
0 946162 59 X *(paperback)*

The first substantial presentation to the English-speaking world of the
work of one of the most important Russian poets of the second half of the
twentieth century. Aygi's free verse is disjunctive, subconscious, anti-
rational; at the confluence of avant-garde European modernism and the
traditional culture of his near-Asiatic homeland. Peter France, translator
of Blok, Pasternak and Brodsky, is the editor of the forthcoming *Oxford
Guide to Literature in English Translation*.

PIERRE CORNEILLE
Horace
*Translated by Alan Brownjohn; introduction and notes by David Clarke*
0 946162 57 3 *(paperback)*

Corneille's powerful drama about the personal cost of national glory, a
work that helped to launch French classical tragedy, is as timely today as
it was in 1640. In the legendary combat between two sets of brothers,
linked by blood and love, to decide a war between Rome and Alba, the
sinister nature of 'patriotism' is laid bare. 'Corneille's rhyming alexan-
drines have been superbly translated into a flexible blank verse which
captures the nuances of meaning, but flows naturally and smoothly. The
language is discreetly updated, dignified but not pompous.' – Maya
Slater, *Times Literary Supplement*

JOHANN WOLFGANG VON GOETHE
Torquato Tasso
*A version by Alan Brownjohn; introduction by T. J. Reed*
0 946162 19 0 *(paperback)*

A play about the moral and social problems of being a patron and being
patronised. In the confrontation between artist and statesman at the cul-
tivated court of Ferrara, Goethe's own experience is fashioned into uni-
versal conflicts. 'The claustrophobic atmosphere Goethe creates by
confining his Romantic character to a Classical play makes the work
structurally a metaphor of its own theme. The translation catches the
breathless spirit of Tasso's visionary soliloquies within a loose blank
verse format and manages to contrast this language with the more regular
and epigrammatic iambic pentameter of the courtly characters he chafes
against.' – Stephen Plaice, *Times Literary Supplement*

OSIP MANDELSHTAM
The Eyesight of Wasps
*Poems translated by James Greene*
*Forewords by Nadezhda Mandelshtam and Donald Davie;*
*introduction by Donald Rayfield; Russian texts in appendix*
0 946162 33 6 *(cased)*    0 946162 34 4 *(paperback)*

One-hundred-and-three poems by one of the giants of twentieth-century Russian poetry. 'Our best Mandelshtam.' – Martin Dodsworth, *The Guardian*. 'Some of Greene's versions work miraculously well . . . throughout I sensed Mandelshtam's own sly and enigmatic ghost.' – Elaine Feinstein, *Sunday Times*

MIODRAG PAVLOVIĆ
The Slavs beneath Parnassus
*Translated with an introduction by Bernard Johnson*
0 946162 20 4 *(paperback)*

This selection of fifty-seven poems by an outstanding living Serbian poet is a modern treatment of themes from classical and Serbian mythology and early Christianity. '. . . simple, moving and brilliant, a reminder of what our own culture no longer possesses.' – Martin Dodsworth, *The Guardian*

FERNANDO PESSOA
The Surprise of Being
*Twenty-five poems; bilingual edition with translations by*
*James Greene and Clara Mafra*
0 946162 24 7 *(paperback)*

The first selection in English to concentrate entirely on poems written in Pessoa's own name, which has been called 'the most confounding of his *personae*'. 'A welcome compilation . . . indispensable.' – J. Pilling, *PN Review*

# Fiction

## THEODOR FONTANE
### Effi Briest
*Translated with an afterword and notes by Hugh Rorrison and
Helen Chambers*
*0 946162 44 1 (paperback)*

A new translation (shortlisted for the Weidenfeld Translation Prize 1996)
of a novel that is now beginning to be critically compared with *Anna
Karenina* and *Madame Bovary* – a story of adultery in Bismarck's Prus-
sia. 'Fontane is a superb eavesdropper . . . the disarming casualness of nar-
rative mode frequently reveals subtexts of extraordinary eloquence . . .
The translators have risen magnificently to the challenge.' – Martin
Swales, *Times Higher Education Supplement*. '. . . a new and superior
English version . . . accurate as no previous translation has been.' – David
Sexton, *The Guardian*

## THEODOR FONTANE
### Cécile
*Translated with an afterword and notes by Stanley Radcliffe*
*0 946162 42 5 (cased)    0 946162 43 3 (paperback)*

The first English translation of the second of Fontane's 'Berlin' novels. At
a fashionable spa in the Harz Mountains an affair develops between an
itinerant civil engineer and the delicate, mysterious wife of a retired army
officer. The dénouement is carried out in the bustling capital of a newly
unified Germany. Fontane confessed to being in love with his female
characters 'for their human qualities, that is, for their weaknesses and
sins.' '*Cécile* is written with wit and a controlled fury and Radcliffe's ele-
gant translation does it superb justice.' – Michael Radcliffe, *The Observer*

## VSEVOLOD GARSHIN
### From the Reminiscences of Private Ivanov *and other stories*
*Translated with an introduction and notes by Peter Henry,
Liv Tudge and others*
*0 946162 08 5 (cased)    0 946162 09 3 (paperback)*

Garshin was Russia's outstanding new writer between Dostoyevsky and
Chekhov. His novellas and short stories include some of the best Russian
war stories and image-rich, densely semiotic narratives like *The Red
Flower* and *The Signal*. This major selection includes almost all his pub-
lished fiction. 'Full of revelations.' – *New Statesman and Society*